FOOTPRINTS ON THE JOURNEY

Footprints on the Journey

ONE YEAR FOLLOWING THE PATH OF
DZOGCHEN MASTER

KHENPO SODARGYE

Wisdom Publications
132 Perry Street
New York, NY 10014 USA
wisdomexperience.org

Library of Congress Cataloging-in-Publication Data
Names: Suodaji, Kanbu, 1962– author.
Title: Footprints on the journey: one year following the path of Dzogchen Master
    Khenpo Sodargye.
Description: New York: Wisdom, [2023]
Identifiers: LCCN 2023033191 (print) | LCCN 2023033192 (ebook) |
    ISBN 9781614298922 | ISBN 9781614299059 (ebook)
Subjects: LCSH: Rnying-ma-pa (Sect)—Doctrines. | Rdzogs-chen. | Suodaji, Kanbu, 1962–
    —Diaries. | Rnying-ma-pa lamas—China—Tibet Autonomous Region—Biography. |
    Rnying-ma-pa lamas—Footprints.
Classification: LCC BQ7662.4 .S865 2023 (print) | LCC BQ7662.4 (ebook) |
    DDC 294.3/420423—dc23/eng/20230801
LC record available at https://lccn.loc.gov/2023033191
LC ebook record available at https://lccn.loc.gov/2023033192

ISBN 978-1-61429-892-2   ebook ISBN 978-1-61429-905-9

28 27 26 25 24
5 4 3 2 1

Artwork by Zhang Hongying. Cover design by Marc Whitaker.
Interior design by Gopa & Ted2, Inc..
Translated from the Chinese by Sally Yuanhong

Contents

Preface

AT LONG LAST, I have finally completed this project. I can't help letting out a deep sigh of relief. The genesis of this diary came from my reading of *Opening the Door to Mind Training* by Lodro Gyaltsen Palzang while I was staying in Xiamen. At that time, I was free from heavy responsibilities at Larung Academy and had the leisure to read and savor this outstanding teaching. But to hoard such a Dharma feast selfishly runs against my sense and sensibility. Why not select a few excellent passages daily and share them? It would benefit me and others, getting twice the results with half the effort. Why not go ahead with it?

Thus, a rudimentary form of this diary started to take shape. Though I initially called it a diary, I did not necessarily make daily entries. Sometimes I had to make up for a few days' contents because of stagnated thoughts. At other times, when my mind bubbled with ideas that rushed over me like pounding waves or galloping wild horses, my pen, trying to keep up with the torrent of inspiration, jotted down in a flowing and bold style many days' accounts in one stretch.

In the early phase of this work, I had ample time to finish articles of a few hundred words quickly, with seemingly little effort; this made me very confident and proud of myself. However, after returning to Larung Academy in the second half of the year, I was immediately ensnared by numerous heavy tasks and trivial chores. My thoughts were jumbled, making it almost impossible to think clearly, even for a single entry. I almost threw away my beloved pens but for the encouragement of many Dharma friends. I managed to continue a little, but only ended up putting this incomplete draft in the bottom drawer, sinking into a deep sleep for nearly two years.

Then, on a bitterly cold winter day—January 7, 2004—the Master of the Three Worlds, the Protector of All Beings, our most beloved Guru Wish-Fulfilling Jewel, His Holiness Jigme Phuntsok Rinpoche, left this world. Utterly caught off guard by his sudden departure, all of us were stricken with sorrow, grieving even more than when losing close relatives. My frail body collapsed at this heavy blow, and the sense of total loss repeatedly struck my already aching heart. Long after the cremation ceremony, I could find nothing to fill my hollow and blank mind. Our teacher had shown us impermanence by the stark reality of his death, which carved indelible marks in our blood, bones, and hearts. I was shaken and made keenly aware of the impermanence of all phenomena as never before.

"Wait no more!" This calling started ringing in my ear, hitting my almost numb heart. It dawned on me that I could not continue making long-term plans and waiting to complete the diary one of these days. Retrieving the dust-covered draft and flipping through the pages absent-mindedly, I caught sight of some teachings from our revered teacher, and then and there, my mind cleared. Now that our teacher had left us, how lucky that I had recorded his instructions, and how precious these entries seemed! If I could make the diary available soon, wouldn't it help us to struggle through this chilly, dark period? Thus, without much fanfare, I made simple edits and sent it off hurriedly, incomplete as it was in many aspects. What fate awaited this diary? I cannot help but worry about its future.

If assessed from the viewpoint of writing, this humble little diary is nothing when lined up against the works of numerous professional authors worldwide. As to a command of the Chinese language, I cannot compare with even an ordinary Han Chinese, let alone with the great masters who are beyond my reach. On all accounts, this diary can be qualified only as a faithful recorder that takes pictures, frame after frame, of the thinking process and daily encounters of an ordinary Buddhist monk. This diary claims no unprecedented idea, profound or complicated theory, or shocking proclamation. Like a casual musical movement spontaneously assembled from pieces, it plays out the vicissitudes of my life over a year. Like an ordinary footprint, it traces a section of my journey in the boundless wilderness of life's desert.

For every practitioner, various experiences arise while treading the spiritual path. Some prefer to keep these accounts to themselves, while here I am, prattling like a melon salesman extolling the sweetness of my fruit. The *Compendium of Trainings* says: "In the bark of sugarcane, there's no sweetness, no matter how one chews on it." Yet I, the "melon salesman," ignoring advice and overrating myself, present this "sugarcane bark" as an offering to readers. If you find it uninteresting, please do not hesitate to leave it on the shelf; I really don't want to be guilty of wasting others' time.

On the other hand, if you like to read something at leisure during practice breaks, leafing through the pages of this diary may be more meaningful than spending time on worldly entertainment that caters to desire, hatred, and delusion. Furthermore, if this little book arouses in you or those around you, even momentarily, respect for the Three Jewels or compassion for sentient beings, all my hard work will not have been in vain.

Here, I make these silent prayers:

> Manifested as a beam of light this diary may be,
> the wild wish for it to match the brilliance of the sun or the
> moon I do not have.
> Only, like an inconspicuous little star in one moonless night,
> may its feeble light shine in the gloomy darkness!

Manifested as soothing coolness this diary may be,
the wild wish for it to sweep away summer heat as the autumn
    gale I do not have.
Only, like a nameless little tree on a sweltering hot day,
may its shade provide cool shelter for beings tormented by
    heat!

Manifested as a medicine this diary may be,
the wild wish for it to be a panacea for all diseases I do not
    have.
Only, like a soothing palliative for the jittery and restless,
may it offer peace and comfort during times of distress!

Oh, wild geese, high in the sky,
flying back north in the spring,
could you please tell me:
Will my wishes ever come true?

I dedicate this book to all my Dharma friends who, like me, will forever
remember our beloved Supreme Guru!

Written with reverence at Larung Buddhist Academy
on the birthday of His Holiness Jigme Phuntsok Rinpoche
January 3, 2004
Sodargye

Translator's Introduction

KHENPO SODARGYE of the Larung Buddhist Academy in Sichuan, China, is a Buddhist scholar, teacher, writer, intellectual, and life ethicist. As one of the most erudite and respected Tibetan teachers of our time, he is a lama who transmits the highest Great Perfection at the world's largest monastic college and, on casual occasions, talks with everyday people about the importance of being kind and upholding worldly ethics. He is a monk equally at home lecturing at top-notch universities worldwide or squatting with scantily-clad aboriginals on the African savannah, learning how to make a fire with two sticks and some dry grass.

Footprints on the Journey contains excerpts from a diary Khenpo kept for a year in 2002, including the six months he spent recuperating from illnesses. The backdrop of this journal is the Tibetan plateau, with its unique geography and culture far removed from that of most Western countries and modern China. Khenpo invites us to see this realm— from hospital staff to a spider, from vast galaxies to a drop of water— just as he does, with candor and tender humor, and at times with a Dzogchen master's sharp analysis. He shares with us his perceptions of and reactions to his world, describing his ups and downs in a way that we can relate to and be inspired by, even if we might not have the fortitude to bargain with a slaughterhouse to ransom condemned yaks or to sit through a sky burial. He shows us how he deals with the chanciness of daily life and how to stay composed and calm when life throws us curveballs.

For instance, one winter in a small Tibetan village Khenpo taught shepherd families in the open air, and when it suddenly started to snow he did not pause or stop. In no time, Khenpo's body was covered in snow flurries, and the pointed pile that accumulated on his head fittingly resembled a pandita's hat. His rapt audience, likewise unfazed, stayed put like rows of snowmen.

All wisdom traditions teach that spiritual instructions are not to be read and then shelved; instead, they must be breathed and lived. *Footprints on the Journey*, created from the diary Khenpo kept from Losar (the Tibetan New Year) through December 11, gives us a glimpse of this theme in Khenpo Sodargye's own voice; we feel we are sitting next to him as he narrates the chapter of his life when he was blossoming into a great spiritual master. Time and time again, we witness his keen grasp of impermanence and the true nature of all phenomena; his profound reverence for the Buddhadharma and spiritual mentors is palpable.

Khenpo said humbly in the preface of his diary:

> Manifested as a beam of light this diary may be,
> the wild wish for it to match the brilliance of the sun or the
> moon, I do not have.
> Only, like an inconspicuous little star in one moonless night,
> may its feeble light shine in the gloomy darkness!

May it be so!

Sally

Snapshots

Life Liberation

I WILL soon be forty, an age, according to Confucius, "when one is no longer confused." With not too many days left, how can I catch the fleeting moments and use them meaningfully? Sages and past spiritual teachers have advised watching one's mind and conduct. If I can apply even one verse to discipline myself, it definitely will be beneficial.

Today is the Tibetan New Year's Day, Losar, and the second day of the Chinese Lunar New Year. An intensely festive mood pervades the streets and neighborhoods, and many people wear traditional stylish Tang outfits to celebrate. Some go to the marketplace to buy holiday treats—live chickens, ducks, fish, shrimp, and birds—for family and friends. But for those poor animals, this festive period is the ultimate doomsday.

As soon as I walked into the local wet market, I saw a shocking scene. A young man grabbed a little quail in a cage and mercilessly stripped off all its feathers, exposing its naked pink body. The poor bird cried in pain, yet its scream was too meek and brief to stop the butcher. Then, in less than a minute, a sharp knife sliced open its body cavity and cut off its head and feet. The hollowed-out body still quivered faintly, its eyes remained wide open on the lopped-off head as if to protest the utterly brutal treatment: "Why? Why?"

I could not bear to look at this scene any longer and bought up the remaining quails, 150 in all. Bringing them into the woods next to the Minnan Buddhist Academy, I released them while reciting lifesaving prayers to bless them. I resolved to continue saving the lives of the captured beings for as long as I could.

Due to a medical condition, I was advised to stay away from the snow-capped Tibetan highland, so I came to the southern city of Xiamen more than a month ago. As a lonely visitor in a strange town, I can't help feeling like a rootless wanderer traveling to the far ends of the earth. How fondly do I miss the days at Larung! On impulse, I called my brother and asked him to place the phone receiver next to the loudspeaker. Soon the melodious chanting at the academy came through the receiver, filling my heart with a deep yearning.

I look forward to early spring at Larung with ice melting, flowers blooming, and green buds emerging! How I wish that the snow and ice would melt and that the warm season of green leaves and blossoms would arrive soon. May beautiful Larung soon enjoy the new season! May the sangha members no longer suffer from the bitter winter, may they bask in the warm sunlight and be showered with the Dharma nectar! May such a day arrive soon! Lama chen!

February 13

Practice Immediately

M ANY lay practitioners today feel trapped by worldly obliga-
tions—parents, children, jobs, family—that cause them constant worry. On the other hand, robe-clad monks and nuns who should
be concentrating on Dharma practice are busying themselves with
building Dharma centers, erecting Buddha statues, or caring for disciples. Preoccupied with these outward good deeds all day, they have
little or no time for inward reflection. I feel this is not a good trend and
worry about it. A genuine Dharma practitioner should give up external
affairs and look internally to realize the mind's true nature, which is the
successful path many past great siddhas have trodden.

In the *Life Story of Milarepa*, there is this passage: Once Jetsun Milarepa was about to leave for his hometown. His teacher, Marpa, reluctantly bidding his student goodbye, imparted this golden advice as
spiritual sustenance:

> My heart son! You must renounce the world and discern the
> supreme Dharma from mundane matters. Otherwise, your
> practice will be impulsive and useless.
>
> My heart son! You should reflect deeply on the samsaric
> suffering whose misery I cannot describe completely, even if
> I grow a hundred tongues and live countless kalpas.
>
> So please don't waste the marvelous Dharma that I have
> taught you.

Keeping these words firmly in his heart, Milarepa practiced accordingly and finally attained complete enlightenment.

Not only do great Buddhist masters feel this way, but also worldly sages know that coveting fame and money wastes valuable time and ultimately comes to nothing. In *The Roots of Wisdom*, it says:

> Striving hard, you seize power and wealth, yet you must give it
> all up eventually—all gains are but losses.
> You may live to be a hundred, yet if you are busy every day,
> you can scarcely say you've lived a single day.

What we call life hinges on this breath and the next. That's it. Just learn to let go of attachment!

February 14

Master's Birthday

TODAY is our precious Guru Jigme Phuntsok Rinpoche's birthday. According to the Tibetan way of counting, he has reached the ripe old age of seventy.

Any amount of compassion or wisdom that arises in students' minds, even for an instant, is a blessing bestowed by the teacher's kind heart. Even without mentioning the incalculable merit our guru has accumulated throughout his numerous lifetimes, he has attracted countless beings onto the Dharma path in this life alone. It would be impossible for me to describe even a mere drop of our guru's ocean of boundless qualities of having perfect wisdom and compassion, keeping pure precepts, and turning the Dharma wheel far and wide.

An old Chinese saying goes: "From ancient times, it has been rare for humans to live to the age of seventy." These days our guru appears to be advancing to senior years and suffering from various illnesses. Yet his efforts to benefit sentient beings, instead of stagnating, are growing stronger. Ignoring his deteriorating health, he still confers blessings on followers from everywhere and continues to plant virtuous seeds in other beings' minds in all possible ways.

Disciples in different locations spontaneously release captive animals on this day, praying that our guru will remain long in this world. Through his blessings, countless lives are spared from sharp murderous knives. Had these creatures known the kindness behind their rescue, how would they express their gratitude? Moreover, upon hearing the holy names of buddhas and sacred mantras recited for them, how would they tell of their eagerness to repay the kindness?

Today, physicians arriving from the United States are treating Rinpoche attentively. I press my palms together in reverence and pray from the bottom of my heart: May our teacher recover swiftly from illness and regain health. May we be blessed with his grace every day. Lama chen!

February 15

The Nurse

THE LITTLE NURSE, who seems incapable of putting even a faint smile on her stiff face, just came in. "How many bowel movements did you have yesterday?" she asked. I've been hospitalized for over a month, and she has asked the same question every day, offering no other greeting. I felt it was pretty ridiculous and replied, "Same. How about some other greeting?" Tilting her dignified head and glaring at me, she walked away.

Thoughts rushed through my mind. But what do I expect?

In the Buddha's previous life, he assumed the responsibilities of doctors and nurses by taking tender care of patients suffering from prolonged illnesses and offering them medicine. Shantideva, a bodhisattva, makes these aspirations in *The Way of the Bodhisattva*: "For all those ailing in the world, until their every sickness has been healed, may I myself become for them the doctor, the nurse, the medicine itself." Many great Buddhist masters have also devoted themselves to benefiting all beings without concern for their own safety or welfare.

Such altruism is not limited to Buddhists; worldly people with high ideals have also voiced their wish to benefit humanity. Du Fu of the Tang dynasty wrote:

How can I build thousands of big houses with plenty of rooms?
I'll use them to shelter all the poor scholars and make them smile
happily. Even if my thatched hut is the only one destroyed by
the elements and I am to die from freezing, I am willing.

I wish Buddha's teachings would penetrate people's minds so that the world will have one ounce more of goodness and one ounce less of ugliness!

February 16

Internet Surfing

THE RAPID and continuous advances in scientific fields have brought dramatic changes to human life. Modern technology products such as mobile phones and computers are now accessible to everyday people, even in remote Tibetan areas. The constraints of time and space disappear with new tools. No matter how distant, people can communicate as if they were next to each other; even ancient peoples seem to come alive on web pages. An adage describes this situation well: without even leaving the house, a scholar knows what is happening in the world.

People are becoming well-informed by using the internet. One after the other, many distinguished Dharma teachers have set up their own websites and discussion forums. Using convenient modern tools, they make Dharma teachings available to lead confused beings onto a path of liberation. Nonetheless, there are also negative influences from the internet that cannot be ignored. The online information is a mixture of good and bad, true and false. Many teenagers, lacking prudent judgment, surf the web all day long. Some Buddhists may even peek into forbidden sites while neglecting their primary task of study, reflection, and meditation on the Dharma. It is worrisome that scientific discoveries are being misused and wasted.

A wise person applies technology skillfully to benefit self and others. On the other hand, a foolish person uses the same technology to commit misdeeds. Just as the *Jewel Heap Sutra* says: "The Buddha told Kashyapa, 'The wise use skillful means to attain liberation, the unwise use clever ways to become shackled.'" This passage applies perfectly to the issue of adopting or abandoning information found on the web.

May people heed this teaching well!

February 17

On Retreat

IT'S BEEN 142 days since I left Larung. Before my departure, 360 practitioners vowed in unison that in the supremely blessed land of Larung, they would devote 142 retreat days to Vajrayana practice, following strictly the retreat manual, which sets at least four to six meditation sessions daily. I had the same aspirations then, but alas, my busy administrative duties and illness thwarted my wishes.

Instead, I have been confined for almost three months in a hospital bed, where I have witnessed the suffering of many patients and heard enough of their miserable shrieks. Some fellow patients of yesterday are escorted away by the Lord of Death today, and who knows how many of today's roommates will be able to enjoy the spring day tomorrow? Unless we take advantage of our rare opportunity to practice, we will be tossed about by karmic force into the rounds of samsara when dying. There will be no protector whatsoever.

Today the 142-day group retreat is completed. This occasion is a feat to commemorate, far more worthy than those elaborate ceremonies for worldly affairs. When the five degenerations flourish, meditating primarily on the mind's true nature is rare, even among seasoned practitioners. Whatever accomplishment these retreatants may have achieved, they have already created tremendous merit.

A sutra states: "Shariputra, if there is a practitioner who listens to Dharma teachings and upholds the ten precepts, and if this same person practices meditation on the mind's nature one-pointedly for just one instant, when comparing the merits of these two activities, the latter is far more superior." If ordinary people strive for earthly gains relentlessly, then how much more effort should spiritual practitioners exert for the liberation of self and others? May all practitioners continue to apply their training on a broader scope!

February 18

Sleep Sparingly

WE SHOULD NOT indulge in oversleeping and laziness. Otherwise, nothing can be accomplished, worldly or spiritual.

Buddha Shakyamuni was reborn as Prince Virtuous Light in one of his previous lives. For many years, to make offerings to the buddhas, he rarely slept and never took breaks except for eating and going to the bathroom.

Geshe Chekawa devoted all his time to Dharma practice and never slept. His master Dromtonpa told him: "You better rest, my son. You'll make yourself ill if the four elements become imbalanced." "Yes, it's nice to be healthy," Geshe Chekawa replied, "but when I think of how difficult it is to find the freedom and advantages of this human life, I have no time to rest." In his life, he recited the mantra of Akshobhya Buddha 900 million times.

Many successful individuals also choose not to waste their priceless time sleeping in bed. The French writer Balzac slept only four hours daily, from 8 pm to midnight. Upon rising, he would write fiercely to use the quiet hours best. With such ongoing diligence, it's no wonder he composed ninety-six masterpieces of universal acclaim, such as the *Human Comedy*.

In *Treasury of Good Advice*, Sakya Pandita says: "The human life span is short. Half of it is spent in quasi-death sleep at night, and the remaining half, plagued by sickness and old age, is not enjoyable either." *The Way of the Bodhisattva* says:

Take advantage of this human boat,
cross over the mighty river of suffering.
This vessel will be hard to find again,
don't be so foolish as to sleep it away!

As spiritual practitioners, we should remember these fine examples and squander no time in drowsiness and sleep.

February 19

Becoming Disillusioned

THIS BUDDHIST ACADEMY is on the outskirts of a coastal city, away from the metropolitan hustle and bustle. It has good weather year round and elegant surroundings full of lush trees, vivid green fields, and flowing brooks. Nameless flowers bloom lavishly on vines and bushes, giving off subtle fragrances. Birds, chirping melodiously in the woods, fly through treetops, reaching the clouds in no time. All these remind me of the sacred places where many Tibetan Buddhist siddhas had practiced. Right here is such a perfect site.

When Lord Atisha had completed his activities in India and Tibet and was about to leave this world, one of his disciples made this pledge: "Master, I promise to practice diligently." The master was displeased and answered: "I hope you will give up chores." The student tried again. "Well then, should I teach?" The teacher responded the same way. The student asked: "How about practicing while teaching?" Again, the same answer. "Then, what should I do?" The master replied: "You should cast aside all the trivialities of this life."

Bearing his teacher's instruction firmly in mind, the disciple cast away all worldly affairs and set off to a quiet forest in Redreng surrounded by magnificent snow-capped mountains. The melting snow sent numerous waterfalls rushing over boulders, nourishing the trees and meadows and sustaining the forest birds and animals.

In the morning, the sun sent warm light from atop the mountains to greet the practitioner and his animal companions. In the evening, with the wind blowing gently, they retired into the night of profound silence. A cool, sparkling mountain spring gave him sweet drinking water, and fresh, tasty wild fruits sustained him. He made contact with no one, nor did he care about any worldly activities. Persistently, he practiced until the end of his life and finally attained a level unreachable by ordinary people.

February 20
Written at the secluded back side of the Minnan Buddhist Academy

Until Tomorrow

LAMA CHEN! If we don't practice the Dharma as soon as possible, when will we get to do it again? No one can confidently say that he will still be living tomorrow. Turning the pages of *The Collection of Deliberate Sayings*, I found these lines: "Who is sure he will live until tomorrow? Today is the time to be ready, for the legions of Death are not on our side."

Stonehouse Qinggong, an ascetic Zen master of the Yuan dynasty, lived in rocky caves for years and had little contact with the outside world. He passed down a collection of mountain poems, each of which diffuses a refreshing valley flair:

> My home among the cliffs is like a tomb,
> barren of even one worldly thought.
> Although I eat food and wear clothes,
> it's as if I were dead but not yet cremated.

Life is like the flame of an oil lamp wavering in the wind; at every moment, it is in danger of being blown out. No one is certain what they will encounter in the next moment, and neither can anyone be sure of waking up the following day. Lord Nagarjuna says in *Letter to a Friend*:

> Life flickers in the flurries of a thousand ills, more fragile than
> a bubble in a stream.

In sleep, each breath departs and comes back in; how won-
drous that we wake up living still!

When a yogi named Damcho, a disciple of Mipham Rinpoche,
was making a forest retreat, no matter what time he woke up during
the night, he would say to himself: "Are you so sure you will live until
tomorrow? Do you truly want to go back to sleep?" And immediately,
he would get up and start prostrations, circumambulation, and other
Dharma practices.

The wise are also acutely aware of the brevity of life. There is a saying: "Finish today's task today; you may not see the sunrise again." In
the *Song of Tomorrow*, Master Wenjia of the Qing dynasty sings: "Tomorrow after tomorrow, too many tomorrows. Waiting always until tomorrow, when will anything be accomplished?"

Pretentious practitioners like myself and others always procrasti-
nate and waste our precious human lives in distractions. Now, having
the masters' instructions, I must urge myself: Abandon all trifle affairs,
practice!

February 23

Wisdom and Compassion

TO SPEAK impressively does not make one an authentic spiritual practitioner; what counts is genuinely turning the mind toward the Dharma while casting away the mundane world.

The great Zen master Damei realized his mind's nature, as pointed out by his teacher Mazu. After that, he retreated to a mountain hut for years. An old friend, Officer Qi An, learned of the master's whereabouts and sent emissaries to cordially invite him out. The Zen master politely declined the offer with these two verses:

> To a ruined, dead tree in the chilly forest,
> many spring seasons have brought no revival.
> Even passing woodcutters heed it not.
> What worth is it for you to pursue me?

And:

> Clothing is plenty from the lotus leaves in the pond.
> Food is abundant among pine berries and flowers.
> Into even deeper woods I'm moving my hut,
> lest it would be exposed again, like the old one.

These verses clearly show that Master Damei has firmly renounced the secular world. Let there be spring flowers and autumn moon; nothing will entice his heart into blossoming or yearning again. All his earthly emotions and sensory pleasures are purified, and he is content with wearing lotus leaves and eating pine berries. This is truly the conduct of great yogis, and I feel deeply humbled when reflecting on it.

Khenpo Chogyal of Serthar, Sichuan Province, was exactly like this. He went to Shiqu to receive teachings from his guru. He cared not about fame, wealth, profit, and power; for decades his dwelling was a shabby room made from wood planks. Although his life was tough, he was carefree and practiced until his final day. Once he said, "With wisdom, an authentic practitioner clings to nothing, and his compassion for sentient beings arises effortlessly. With wisdom and compassion, the essence of the sutras and tantras is within reach; without them, one could talk impressively about altruism but will scheme for personal gain at the slightest temptation." The omniscient Longchenpa also says: "Your training should bring a change in you as noticeable as if you had worn your clothes the wrong way." Hence, no amount of talk could mean anything without wisdom and compassion. Bear this in mind!

February 24

Be Diligent

THE SUN BEAMS shafts of warm light down through the leaves of a tall arbor tree, and the jasmine tea in my cup exudes a delicate fragrance. Sitting on the balcony in this refreshing setting, I idly hold a book but cannot concentrate. The neighboring Xiamen Middle School opens its new term today. Students wearing bright uniforms pour onto the campus, driving off yesterday's quietness. My mind, easily distracted by my surroundings, also starts rushing around.

This middle school is well equipped and has modern facilities—brand new buildings, big open sports fields, colorful gardens, and kind and capable teachers. Students conduct physical exercises in unison and play actively and cheerfully during recess. Unexpectedly, my mind drifts back to my lovely days at the Zong Ta Middle School, my alma mater.

At that time, modern facilities were non-existent, and we wore only ragged clothes. Yet we were happy kids all the same. Over time, three out of my seven former roommates and dear friends have passed away. In my dreams, I often revisit our tender youth together, only to wake up finding no trace of those blissful times! Even though I do not know which realms my classmates were reborn in, I sincerely hope they enjoy happiness and peace. *Om Mani Padme Hum Hri!*

I am now a man of over forty. Even if I live into my sixties, only twenty rounds of seasons remain. By chance, we came into this world, and sadly our number of years is never long enough. Time moves on silent footsteps and never pauses, even for a moment. To a diligent person, the passage of time brings wisdom and strength; to the indolent, only regrets and an aching void.

If not today, when is the time to be diligent?

February 25

Purification Practice

TODAY FALLS within the "month of miracles" in the Tibetan calendar. Many Dharma adherents perform virtuous deeds this month, such as fasting, circumambulation, prostration, liberating lives, and so on. It is also the Lantern Festival Day in Han China, usually celebrated by lighting lanterns, setting off firecrackers, and performing lion dances festively.

To make their reunions with friends and relatives "more cheerful," some fools entertain at the expense of other beings' lives. For the sake of celebratory feasting, many beings lose their lives in restaurants when fried in oil or boiled in water—a bloody purgatory played out right here in the human realm.

> Like humans, animals feel pain when hurt.
> Unlike humans, they can only weep silent tears.

Let us practice purification for the woefully slaughtered beings and the evil perpetrators!

In *Collection of Good Deeds*, Chagme Rinpoche imparts this simple pith instruction: "Visualize Vajrasattva at the crown of your head. From him, numerous Vajrasattvas emanate, each sitting on top of the head of each individual, living or dead. Recite the *Hundred-Syllable Mantra* as well as possible, and visualize nectar flowing down from Vajrasattva's body, cleansing the obscurations of yourself and all others. Recite the mantra another 108 times, and then visualize that Vajrasattva dissolves into light and melts into yourself and all others. Meanwhile, recognize the purification process, Vajrasattva, and you are all empty, devoid of intrinsic existence. Abide in the state of emptiness momentarily. This confession method encompasses relative and absolute truths and can purify even the incalculable downfalls from previous lives."

Beyond today, we can continue this practice to purify the non-virtues of our family members and others daily, which is necessary and very convenient.

February 26

Reflecting Inward

THE OMNISCIENT Longchenpa says in *The Great Chariot: A Treatise on Finding Comfort and Ease in the Nature of Mind*:

> In brief, one should realize the unchanging thusness of the mind's luminosity and see that all phenomena are but labels, empty of inherent existence. By practicing ardently, one can completely transmute or purify the illusory appearances of imputative grasping. Arriving at the primordial state, one perfects the mastery of a pure land of the inexhaustible ornamental wheel of enlightened body, speech, and mind.

This teaching is the core of all the Dharmas and the essence of the buddhas of all times. Summing up the 84,000 Buddhist gateways into one sentence, the omniscient Longchenpa left it to destined future generations. Now that we've met this treasure, unsurpassable by all the wish-fulfilling jewels, how fortunate we are!

If one turns the mind inward and abides in it, the mind's primordial luminosity will reveal itself. Otherwise, seized by dualistic grasping, one becomes confused and perverted, and endless aftermaths ensue. Piling life's baggage on one's shoulders—food and clothing, love or hate, honor or disgrace, gain or loss, right or wrong, success or failure—is a sure way to open wide the highway to samsara.

The unconventional Zen master Shi De of the Tang dynasty once said:

Not knowing the mind's true nature, one always seeks fame
   and wealth.
Having gained fame and wealth, one appears careworn and
   haggard.
Not to mention those who failed at the game, wasting their
   lives all along!

Again, the master, seeing that ordinary people are still oblivious to the doctrines and labor painstakingly for minuscule gains, teaches:

Unmindful are worldly folks, always immersed in sensual
   pleasures.
Arising in my heart is compassion when beholding these
   beings.
Worrying about their suffering, how can I not feel sad?

The master's earnest compassion is obvious. But alas, as the saying goes:

Yearning for love, the flower on the bank sheds its petals,
   yet the heartless brook heeds not and babbles on.

No wonder the Zen master can only sigh deeply in vain! May the master's genuine guidance not dissipate into nothingness as time passes!

February 28

Life and Death

LIFE, as composed by musicians, is the faint melody of flutes drifting from a remote place. As penned by writers, it is a refreshing spring in the desert. As seen by sociologists, it is a charging train of desires. Life, as filled with poetic charm as it seems, remains unfathomable. In modern times, humans have made great strides in material civilization, yet like the eternal riddle of ancient Egypt, life itself remains an impassable chasm for most Westerners.

Westerners' comprehension of human consciousness was tentative and incomplete until Walter Evans-Wentz first published an English translation of *The Tibetan Book of the Dead* in 1927. This book, a classic of Tibetan Buddhism taught by Padmasambhava, reveals the mystery of living and dying according to meditative experiences. Thanks to its rendition into many languages, it has attracted significant attention worldwide, and people can now ponder the process of living and dying from a Tibetan Buddhist perspective.

In 1973 Ram Dass founded a hospice center to provide services for terminal cancer and AIDS patients, where staff members help patients to find hope in hopeless situations. He once visited a dying patient named Bruce in San Francisco and read the teachings from *The Tibetan Book of the Dead* to him: "Escape not from the pains and confess your mistakes. Learn to be calm and at peace. Slowly you will recognize the innate luminosity of your mind . . ." Guided by Ram Dass, Bruce's twisted, agonized face gradually relaxed, and he made a tranquil exit.

What baffles Westerners the most is that nearly every elderly

Tibetan can be deemed an expert in hospice care. From a young age, Tibetans learn how to face death squarely, and, with training, many practitioners have long regarded death as a turning point to spring into liberation when discarding the fleshly body. On the contrary, Westerners often feel completely lost on their deathbeds and can only plead to medical doctors for help. Comparing these two attitudes, we must say that Tibetans are lucky.

We are forever in debt to Guru Padmasambhava for teaching us how to unlock the secret of life and death. It indeed is a most precious spiritual legacy!

March 1

Knowing Not

O H NO, the horrible backache is attacking me again. Sickness is anything but merciful. It pounces, leaving me in no mood to enjoy the pleasant spring days, whether warm or chilly, cloudy or cloudless.

A person becomes most vulnerable to the thought of death during illness. Perhaps I'll die today! Who knows if I can finish translating *The Great Biography of Shakyamuni Buddha, the White Lotus?* Will *The Great Chariot: A Treatise on Finding Comfort and Ease in the Nature of Mind* start and end well? As I have not been mindful of death, I have wasted much of my life. Now that old age is creeping in, I can't help feeling my days are numbered, just like the sun setting beyond the western hills.

To encourage myself, I read a song of realization by Zen Master Hong Zhi of the Southern Song dynasty:

> Dharma bliss is my sustenance and compassion is my dwelling.
> Faith in the Buddha is my destination; this body of mine is
>   merely on loan.
> Being mindful is my sole endeavor; I have no time to spare for
>   earthly affairs.

Can I accomplish all that he said? It is tough!

March 3

Hit Me

TO BRING ABOUT their disciples' sudden revelations, great masters throughout history have, at times, employed unconventional training methods in addition to gentle ways.

As a disciple of Tilopa, Naropa had to undergo twelve minor hardships followed by twelve major hardships. Finally, Tilopa grabbed Naropa's throat with his left hand, and with his right hand he took off one of his sandals and hit his disciple on the forehead. Naropa passed out. When he came to, all the qualities of his teacher had arisen in him. The teacher's wisdom and the disciple's mind had become one in realization.

At age seventeen, Zen master Liao Yi of the Song dynasty formally visited Master Gao Feng. He was given the pith instruction of meditating on "all phenomena are converged to be one." One day, seeing snowflakes falling from pine branches, Liao Yi was inspired to write a poem and submitted it to his teacher. Explaining nothing, the master lifted a wooden stick and hit the student, knocking him down into a deep ravine. With painful wounds all over his body, Liao Yi reflected on the nature of the mind and finally reached the stage beyond all concepts and elaborations. He left these beautiful lines:

> Gone swiftly are the snows covering the vast land, once the
>   sun appears.
> Gone are my fixations on this or that, once my doubts about
>   the buddhas vanish.

When Zen master Huang Bo took Lin Ji as his disciple, he hit him with sticks sixty-one times, making Lin Ji the most outstanding Zen master in generations. There is a saying about Zen schools: "The Lin Ji school is like a war general, while the Cao Dong school is like a field farmer." While carrying on the lineage tradition, Lin Ji also developed his unique Zen style that surpassed even his teacher's.

When, if ever, will my guru hit me on the head?

March 4

Auspicious Dream

T HE CLOCK had just struck six when I woke up. I had a good
dream last night. As an ordinary person, I couldn't help feeling
overjoyed, even knowing that all dreams are illusory. I hesitated about
writing down my dream, but in the end, I did.

This is the third time I dreamed of Ju Mipham Rinpoche since leaving Chengdu. The first dream happened when I was in a hospital, in
which I received a transmission to teach the *Commentaries on Distinguishing Dharma and Dharmata*. In the second dream in the same hospital,
Mipham Rinpoche gave me the transmission of *Distinguishing the Middle and the Extremes* and the *Gateway to Knowledge*. Upon waking, I was so
proud of myself and could barely hold back my urge to immediately
translate or teach the transmissions I had just received.

Last night, Mipham Rinpoche appeared as three different persons
in turn. When the last one came, I clearly sensed that this emanation
must be Mipham Rinpoche. He looked like a Kham layman in his forties, with gleaming black hair and eyes brimming with vigor. He had
thick, dark eyebrows and snow-white teeth; a rosy tint infused his
tanned face. Wearing blue Tibetan brocade, he settled pleasantly to
the left side of my bed. A deep reverence arose in my heart, and I felt
that he was the wisdom embodiment of all the buddhas and bodhisattvas. He seemed amicable, and I sought his advice on the questions I
always had. When I woke up, I could still feel the warmth of his body,
and I dared not touch where he had been moments ago.

Some people disapprove of talking about dreams. Ridgzin Jigme

Lingpa once said: "A good dream will never come back again after being disclosed." Our revered Guru Jigme Phuntsok Rinpoche also taught this: "A tiger can leap quite far, but a frog just cannot follow suit." It seems that talking about one's dreams is not a good idea. Anyway, now I have, and that's it.

Here, I have described only the good dreams that came to me once in a blue moon. Should I recount all my bad dreams, they would be like long filthy foot wraps.

March 6

Lotus Flower

HERE I AM in this southern city, far away from my hometown. All alone in a strange land, I am often engulfed by loneliness, having no friends or kin to turn to. Only the lotus pond facing the front door greets me every day. No sooner have I seen the lotus leaves as barely pointed buds then they become a full panel of lush green. Lotus flowers with a riot of color—deep red, pink, creamy white—blossom gracefully and shapely. As I was feasting my eyes on this poetic and picturesque scenery, I suddenly noticed a lotus flower in one corner. Its head drooped low as if overladen by sorrow and weariness, totally unaffected by the spectacular spring.

"Little lotus flower, why are you so sad?"

"There was a dewdrop yesterday. We got along so well, and I adore it very much. But today, the sun snatched my dewdrop away. Now the bliss we enjoyed together is all gone, and I am utterly miserable and cannot extricate myself from this feeling. Oh, how I hate the sun! Why must he plunder my little dewdrop?"

So the little lotus flower bared her soul to me. I was at a loss as to what to offer. Perhaps she could use some of Mipham Rinpoche's blessings. Finding my favorite passage from Mipham Rinpoche's teachings, I read it to her: "The fools, thinking that external factors cause all happiness and suffering, are forever distracted in wanting and rejecting and lost in the waves of craving and aversion. The wise, knowing that the source of all happiness and suffering is the self, always reflect inward and guard against disturbing emotions."

After listening to my explanation, the little lotus flower felt better. She let go of her clinging to the dewdrop and no longer held a grudge against the sun. Moreover, she took refuge in the Three Jewels of Buddhism, and her inner strength grew daily. Even though she was withering away, she felt confident and enriched. I was joyous to witness her transformation. The blessings of the Three Jewels are inconceivable! When I was ready to be discharged, the little flower declared her firm resolution: "I will study the Buddha's teaching and practice my best!"

In reality, the little lotus flower is Dr. He, who gives me medicine and a shot every day. The dewdrop is her boyfriend, and the sun is her sister. Can people find their own images in this story?

March 11
At Xiamen 174 Hospital

Generating Bodhichitta

WHATEVER WE DO, we must do it by arousing bodhichitta first. The *Sutra Requested by Maitreya* says: "Maitreya, water that has flowed into the ocean will not dry up even after many kalpas. Maitreya, any positive actions done with bodhichitta intention will never be exhausted until one reaches the highest and perfect realization."

If we bring about bodhichitta, everything we do will bear merit, even neutral activities. The *Avatamsaka Sutra* says: "Having aroused bodhichitta, all activities of body, speech, and mind become meaningful and virtuous, even for a distracted person." The sutra also lists 250 examples to aptly describe the excellence of bodhichitta.

Bodhichitta is the quintessential butter of the wisdom milk that comes from studying, contemplating, and meditating; it is the cool moonlight that dispels the heat of sentient beings' aggravation; it is the brilliant rising sun that drives away the darkness of ignorance; it is the ultimate vehicle that leads beings toward liberation. Maudgalyayana, even with his supernatural power, could not extinguish a lamp that a poor woman had offered with bodhichitta. After a long retreat, Asanga finally had a vision of Bodhisattva Maitreya only because he had aroused genuine bodhichitta. Indeed, the benefits of bodhichitta are just too numerous to count!

March 13

It's Impermanent

AT THIS MOMENT, the once brilliant and outstanding Mr. Sun sits beside me, holding photos of his youthful self. Tears stream down his cheeks as he looks at them, like crystal beads falling from a broken mala string. He feels sad that he has lost his glorious prime and will never be young again. All his jubilant years, like a river rushing forward, are now gone beyond recall.

The poem *Burying Flowers* by Lin Daiyu in *Dream of the Red Chamber* comes to mind:

> Spring is ending, and the flowers are wilting one by one—
> that is the time when beauty must grow old and die.
> Once spring departs and the fair maiden meets her doom,
> who will notice the fallen blossoms and the dead beauty?

I sense this must be an intimate portrayal of Mr. Sun's mood. Too bad he has not studied Buddhism and does not know how to alleviate his sorrow with wisdom. Like the tidal waves, his gloomy feeling can only surge higher when given free rein. How lamentable!

Everything—youth, wealth, relationships, even life—is ephemeral. The poet Bai Juyi says: "Be not proud, young fellows, you will soon become white-haired old gents!" Try as we might, we couldn't hold on to youth as life and death march on. It will be regrettable if we fail to devote our vigorous years to studying the Dharma. Mipham Rinpoche says:

Youth is momentary and wealth is fickle; life is like being in the jaws of the Lord of Death. Yet many people still ignore Dharma practice. Alas, how disconcerting is their behavior!

I should explain these teachings to Mr. Sun. He's intelligent; I'm sure he'll come to terms with his perceived predicament. Closing my book, I decided to have a good talk with him.

March 15

Meritorious Activities

PEOPLE with kind hearts enjoy doing good deeds, whether they believe in Buddhism or not. For instance, they help build schools and support people experiencing poverty in rural areas. As for religious activities, they donate money to temples and monastic communities or pay respect by offering prostrations to deities.

Those who have done bad things may also engage in virtues to ease their conscience. Chinese Lunar New Year's Eve is when folks pack into local temples to offer incense and prostrations. Police and fire trucks stand by for fear of fires in overcrowded conditions. People come in continuously, and many have to wait in long lines that go on for several blocks. Even the skyrocketing admission fees do not discourage the arriving crowds.

Rejoicing in this, I recall a passage from the *Mahaparinirvana Sutra*: "Some people may offer the seven precious substances, beds, and food to all the buddhas throughout their lives. Alternatively, others may generate bodhichitta in the mindstream, even for an instant— the latter would reap more outstanding merit." Thus, just arousing the thought of bodhichitta is immensely meritorious, let alone applying bodhichitta in real action! As the *Sutra of the Maiden Excellent Moon* says: "If the merit of merely wishing to help others knows no bounds, what is there to say of benefiting others with actual deeds?"

Therefore, spiritual practitioners should not seek superficial merit. Instead, arouse the altruistic mind of bodhichitta. To practice it even once a day is vastly worthwhile!

March 16

Profound Practice

MANY Dharma practitioners are keen to request exalted teachings—Mahamudra, Great Madhyamaka, Great Perfection, Yamantaka, etc. In addition, they are eager to seek out eminent monks, high tulkus, and famous masters. These fans of profound Dharma feel that by so doing, an extraordinary realization will dawn on them accordingly. Well, this may not be the case. Whatever practices one requests should match well one's own capacity. Unless one meets the basic required training in the first place, no accomplishment will ensue.

Gyalwa Yangonpa, one of the foremost disciples of Sakya Pandita, is a well-known siddha in Tibetan history. He says: "People usually dash after profound Dharma practices while feeling dissatisfied with lower ones. They behold the high, unfathomable practices with wonder and attention but neglect to check if their minds are ready. Although one could engage in the practice of Great Perfection, it will affect nothing because a practitioner of Great Perfection must be a suitable vessel for it. I have witnessed that teachings as valuable as a fine steed are babbled by people less worthy than a dog. They are running counter to the Dharma but are unwilling to practice. What they say is no different from the melody of an appealing rapper or the verbatim repetition of a clever parrot. When one receives the instructions, one should practice appropriately and let them thoroughly permeate oneself. Failing to do so is like combining two immiscible liquids that don't mix. If the essential instruction does not rise beyond hollow words, the fruition of Dharma practice will never manifest."

Thus, ensure that we saturate our minds and actions with the instructions. The Dharma is not to be used as an ornament or asset to brag about. In *Sakya Lekshe*, it says: "The fool shows off knowledge by talking; the wise stores away knowledge in the heart. A wheat straw floats on the water; a precious jewel sinks to the bottom."

Do not covet other perceived lofty paths when embarking on a spiritual path. Rather, start from square one and proceed in a thorough and solid manner.

March 17

My Mother

M Y MOTHER reminded me on the phone today that I have been away from Larung for 160 days. Every day she thinks about her son living in a distant place.

Like all mothers, my mom paid dearly for my upbringing and spiritual growth. Throughout many rough years, she endured humiliation and burdens that reflected her extreme tenacity and kind heart. Once, when I was two years old, I suddenly became ill. My fever wouldn't drop and I was on the verge of dying. My mom, carrying me on her back, trudged one step after another toward the county town many kilometers away. For two full days and nights, she walked non-stop. The number of times she stumbled and the difficulties she met on the road were uncountable. In the grip of the Lord of Death, I was unconscious until, finally, I managed to break free from the ordeal. It was only then that a smile appeared on my mother's face.

In my childhood, every night after dinner with the whole family sitting around a fire pit, my mom would start her daily homework: reciting *The Aspiration Prayer to Be Born in the Pure Land of Great Bliss*. With the fire casting a reddish glow on her blooming young face, I was struck with a sense of pure awe, as if beholding the immaculate goddess Tara in person. Her vivid recitation and chanting were like melodies coming from the Dakini Land, reverberating on and on in our tent. This subtle influence led to my early understanding of Buddhism. Whenever I hear or read *The Aspiration Prayer to Be Born in the Pure Land of Great Bliss*, my mother's chanting voice resounds in my ears. Thanks to her, I memorized the entire prayer and remember it to this day.

When my mom was still relatively young, her white porcelain face had a reddish tint, her eyes were like jet-black jewels, and her teeth were as white as snow. One day I went herding with her on the mountainside. The trees grew lavishly up there and colorful flowers dotted the verdant pasture. We played hide and seek, and when I spotted her hiding among the flowers, I felt she was just as beautiful as the divine maiden. Perhaps that's the meaning of the Han Chinese proverb: "Never does a son see his own mother as ugly; never does a dog see its own master as poor." These days, the carving knife of time has chiseled deep lines on my mother's face. Her cheeks are sunken and her teeth have fallen out. Her legs are almost crippled, and she can only move her heavy body with a cane. No one would believe me if I described her youth's agility and stunning beauty. Indeed, time shows no mercy to anyone!

The kindness of parents is inconceivable. The Buddha recounts our parents' many acts of kindness in the *Sutra about the Deep Kindness of Parents and the Difficulty of Repaying It*. Master Atisha also teaches that respecting and supporting one's parents is no different from practicing emptiness, which has compassion as its essence.

A Tibetan proverb says: "As flowing water is the mother's heart, as rocky stone is her son's heart." A mother's heart is as tender as water, while her son's is as hard as a rock. When we finally appreciate our parents' sacrifices and want to pay them back and look after them, they have already left this world.

The trees long for calmness, but the wind will not subside.
The son wishes to serve his parents, but they are already gone.

Therefore, while our parents are still alive, we should respect and pay attention to them.

A thread moves in a mother's loving hand,
making a garment for her traveling son.
With all of her affection, she is sewing and sewing,
worrying he'll ever be roving and roving.
Who dares to say that the heart of an inch-long grass
can ever repay a debt as enduring as the warm sun?

The most significant way to repay a mother's kindness is to lead her to embrace Buddhism and arouse her faith in the Three Jewels. What comforts me is that my mother has become a devout Buddhist and taken monastic ordination, which is my little accomplishment in filial piety. Dear mom, please do not worry too much about this undutiful son of yours. Just concentrate on your recitation of the Buddha's name and prayers to the Three Jewels. I'll be back home as soon as I recover from my illness.

March 18

Advice and Encouragement

AS PRACTITIONERS, besides constantly paying attention to our minds, we should also help people connected to us to know the Dharma. For instance, we can encourage our family members, friends, and colleagues to take refuge, study Buddhism, or even enter the monastic order. Many have tried but have given up later, seeing no results after one or two attempts. This attitude also accounts for our failure to integrate bodhichitta into our mental continua.

When Buddha Shakyamuni was a bhikshu named the Power of Diligence in a previous life, it took him 84,000 years (at a time when beings had long life spans) to advise Prince Auspicious Treasure to abandon evil, adopt good, and take refuge in Buddhism. During that period, the bhikshu often sat on the steps of the prince's garden gate, tolerating unjustified public insults. Despite suffering enough of the prince's arrogance and rudeness, the bhikshu assiduously persisted and never lost heart. He finally moved the prince, who began to embrace Buddhism with unshakable faith.

The *Ornament of the Mahayana Sutras* says:

> With matchless diligence, bodhisattvas bring sentient beings
> to full maturity.
> Untiringly for eons, bodhisattvas strive to kindle even a single
> virtue in another's mind.

The omniscient Longchenpa also says: "Even if only one being remains in samsara, I'm willing to stay here and strive tirelessly to bring that one being to liberation. With utmost courage, I'm willing to spend hundreds of thousands of eons, if that's what it takes, to kindle one good thought in one sentient being." As Mahayana students who follow in the Buddha's footsteps and assume the Tathagata family tradition, let us act likewise.

The merit of causing bodhichitta to arise in another being's mind is tremendous. The *Four Hundred Verses of Madhyamaka* says: "If we compare the merit of building the highest stupas in the world with that of causing bodhichitta to arise in one being's mind, the latter is far superior." But it's easier said than done. I have been talking about Buddhism to my doctors here since my hospitalization but have converted no one. How embarrassing!

March 19

Fleeting Time

PEOPLE LIKE to think of time in terms of day and night. I prefer to imagine it as a river of no return. Standing on a river bank, Confucius sighed: "That which passes is like this river, flowing unceasingly, day and night!" The philosopher Heraclitus said: "No man ever steps in the same river twice." The sages all emphasize the preciousness of time. Indeed, just like a rushing river, no moment will ever come back once it's gone, whether splendid or ordinary, happy or sad. Humans can live only once; thus, pondering how to use our time is crucial.

Finding time every day, even ten minutes, to memorize one stanza or take note of a koan is always beneficial for all practitioners. The renowned Chinese writer Lu Xun once said: "I am no genius; I only make full use of time. When people are having coffee, I'd rather be reading or writing." So long as we are unable to bend time backward, we should live every moment of our lives fully. Otherwise, on our deathbed, we will be overcome with remorse for having wasted our precious life. Like squeezing every bit of water out of a wet sponge, let us use every minute and every second on meaningful projects; let us not squander our time on distractions.

March 20

Mental Offerings

MAKING mental offerings is an easy and laudable practice for those trained in concentration and visualization. The following provides specific steps:

> With a steady mind, imagine that you hold many wondrous gifts and offer them to Buddha Shakyamuni or other victorious ones. If you excel in visualization, picture vast objects of veneration filling the whole space: lineage masters, buddhas of all times and directions, and a massive assembly of bodhisattvas and noble sanghas. The *Sutra of Jewel Chest* and the *Avatamsaka Sutra* explains: "Visualize a multitude of offerings in your hands. Offer them to the Buddha before you and to many other buddhas and enlightened beings in the universe."

Additionally, imagine that limitless sentient beings of the six realms join you in offering superb gifts: fine food, the seven riches of a universal monarch, clouds of flowers, heavenly music, divine canopies, and celestial clothing, as well as all varieties of holy incense, fragrant balms, burning incense, and powdered incense. Moreover, offer all kinds of lamps: butter lamps, oil lamps, and lights with aromatic oils, visualizing the wick of each lamp to be as tall as Mount Meru and the quantity of filling to be equal in volume to the waters of the great sea. Imagining all manner of gifts such as these, make offerings repeatedly.

Mipham Rinpoche teaches: "When making mental offerings, first establish faith and devotion. Then, one-pointedly imagine making limitless offerings as cloud banks while recognizing that none has any inherent existence." Hence, rather than engaging in trickery or deception to garner valuables as gifts to spiritual masters, it would be far better to make mental offerings with a pure mind.

Making offerings is an antidote to our stinginess, which pleases buddhas and bodhisattvas. Buddhist adherents always aspire to repay the fourfold kindnesses—kindness coming from one's parents and teachers, the Three Jewels, one's country, and sentient beings—and to relieve the sufferings in the three lower realms. But should one harm other living beings in the name of offerings to buddhas and bodhisattvas, it would be a perverted act confusing cause and effect. So let us take a few minutes daily to make mental offerings with a mind arising from innate purity.

The above practice is one skillful method among many others to accumulate the two merits of wisdom and compassion. How wonderful!

March 22

Four Powers

IN GELUG, Nyingma, or other schools of Tibetan Buddhism, every purification practice entails the four antidotal powers. Buddhists of other regions may consider it a Tibetan approach and inapplicable to them. But such a notion misses the big picture.

The Chinese Buddhist Tripitaka has many accounts of the four powers. For instance, the sutra *Teaching on the Four Factors* says: "Oh Bodhisattva Maitreya, if bodhisattvas possess four factors, they will overcome their accumulated misdeeds. What are these four? They are the power of regret, the power of remedial action, the power of resolution, and the power of reliance. The power of regret is to feel intense remorse for your non-virtuous actions. The power of remedial action is to put great effort into virtuous deeds. The power of resolution is to pledge and refrain from any similar non-virtuous action. The power of reliance is to take refuge in the Buddha, Dharma, and Sangha and not to forsake bodhichitta."

Moreover, the recitation of the Vajrasattva mantra has been described in detail in the *Sutra of Three Wrathful Ways of Taming*. Therefore, both Tibetan Buddhism and Chinese Buddhism contain the practice of confession with four antidotes that, if followed correctly, will purify innumerable non-virtues. If, due to tenacious habits built up in the past, one is still unable to stop taking lives or telling lies, one should sincerely recite the Vajrasattva mantra every day to strengthen the practice.

People these days constantly commit unethical acts, but very few are alert enough to repent truthfully. Maitreya's *Sutra of the Lion's Roar Requested* says: "The fool commits evil actions and knows not how to confess; the wise repent faults and become free from negative karma."

May everyone be mindful of the purification practice amid the distractions of daily life!

March 24

Sustained Effort

THE SPIRITUAL JOURNEY is a protracted and arduous process. Longchenpa says: "Spiritual practice cannot rely on only a few days' work; it takes a long-term struggle and commitment." If we practice diligently and persistently for an extended period, we can build up our willpower and create stocks of merit.

When I was a child there was an aunt named Drala who was young, pleasing, and devoted to Buddhism. She once made a pilgrimage to Lhasa with local villagers and pledged to her teacher that every day she would perform one hundred prostrations, read the *Aspiration Prayer to Be Born in the Pure Land of Great Bliss* once, and recite the Vajrasattva mantra ten thousand times. That was thirty years ago when religions suffered ruthless destruction. In that horrific period, one might recite mantras or read sutras silently without getting caught, but prostrations posed a bigger problem. Besides doing them at home, while herding she also tried to accumulate repetitions in mountain caves and always asked me to stand guard for her. When no one was around, I would remind her: "It's time for you to do prostrations!"

Time flies, and thirty years have passed when I met her again last July in my hometown. I experienced many changes during this period, such as studying and becoming a monk. As for Drala, life had left unforgiving marks on her face. Reminiscing about the old days, I asked her: "Are you still doing prostrations and recitations?" She answered: "Certainly. I've never stopped. Even when I missed them during bouts of severe illness, I always tried to make it up after recovery. Now that I have free time, I can recite even more mantras."

I asked, "Through all these years, how many prostrations and mantra recitations have you done?" She replied, "I just keep practicing and have not bothered to count." I made a quick mental calculation. Conservatively, in the past thirty years, Drala could have done at least 1,095,000 prostrations, read the *Aspiration Prayer to Be Born in the Pure Land of Great Bliss* 10,950 times, and recited the Vajrasattva mantra 109,500,000 times. These numbers may seem astronomical to many, yet Drala is merely an ordinary Tibetan, neither famous nor the most diligent. She has maintained her practice for thirty years with the willpower of grinding an iron pestle down to a needle, which is genuinely praiseworthy.

These days some practitioners can't wait to flaunt their completion of one cycle of 500,000 preliminaries, lest others will not know. Drala, on the other hand, cares not for recognition but only for doing her work steadfastly. Isn't that remarkable? Checking my progress, I noted that while I have made pledges before my master, I have not practiced authentically. People address me as a lama, but I am no better than the average person. Shouldn't I blush with shame?

There is an ancient saying:

> In one jump, even a superior steed cannot reach a distance
> of ten jumps.
> An inferior horse running continuously for ten days reaches
> far ahead—
> success comes from making consistent efforts unremittingly.

Every practitioner should cultivate such a spirit of perseverance. Every ounce of effort will produce an ounce or more of the result.

March 26

Bright Moonlight

THE LAST GLOW in the western sky vanished with the setting sun, and silence was everywhere. As the darkness thickened, I looked forward to enjoying a peaceful spring night alone, which turned out to be wishful thinking. A bright full moon appeared in the high void, sprinkling a fine layer of silver dust over houses, trees, and the garden. A poem came to my mind:

> A thousand waters reflect a thousand moons,
> an utterly cloudless sky reaches ten thousand miles.

This round and bright face appears in lakes, rain puddles, and washbasins as if screaming to be picked up—no wonder the folklore about monkeys trying to rescue the moon fallen into a pond.

Indeed, no matter how many water containers are on the ground, all will reflect the same radiant moon as long as the water surfaces are clean and calm. Similarly, regardless of how many people there are on Earth, as long as they think of the Buddha with a pure mind, the Buddha will come to them to bestow blessings, dispel suffering, and bring happiness.

The *Jewel Heap Sutra* says: "Should anyone think of the Buddha with faith, the Buddha is there, right in front of them, constantly granting his blessings and dispelling harms." The *King of Samadhi Sutra* also says: "Those who—while walking, sitting, standing, or sleeping—recollect the moon-like Buddha will always be in Buddha's presence and attain vast happiness." People may wonder: How could the Buddha come to us the moment we think about him? Such manifestation is made possible by our pure minds and the power of Buddha's great compassion.

A dutiful Buddhist would feel ashamed to let a day go by without thinking of the Lord Buddha Shakyamuni even once. Continually reading and reflecting on scriptural passages will enhance wisdom and oust obstacles. However, if we let the water vessel of our faith turn upside down, the Buddha moon will have no way to reflect on us.

March 28

No Ending

THE BUDDHA SAYS all sentient beings have previously been our own mothers and fathers, but many people find this notion improbable and even impossible. Putting aside the argument for the existence of past lives, if this were true, how could we ever exhaust all sentient beings, as their number is simply innumerable?

However, the conclusions reached by the ordinary sense faculties—eye, ear, nose, tongue, body, and mind—are not valid in the ultimate sense. The *King of Samadhi Sutra* says:

> The eyes, the ears, and the nose are unreliable,
> the tongue, the body, and the mind are unreliable.
> If ordinary senses could be relied on,
> what need would there be for noble ones to teach?

Only with transcendent wisdom can the true nature of all phenomena be known. Without relying on Buddha's profound insight, no amount of ordinary conceptual thinking will be able to penetrate the essence of a myriad of appearances.

Likewise, the notion of time without beginning is difficult to grasp with ordinary faculties. In *Letter to a Friend*, the sublime Nagarjuna says: "Should the bones we had through our past lives be piled up, they would be as high as Mt. Meru. Should we try to count our bodies with balls of clay the size of juniper berries, we would run out of earth to count." Since time immemorial, we have lived incalculable lives in samsara, and the number of times we had relationships of love, hate, or non-involvement with one another is also countless. The *Sages' Nirvana Sutra* says: "Were this great earth made into pellets as small as peas, to count the number of times a being had been my father and mother would use up the whole earth before I could finish counting."

Hence, until we have carefully studied and reflected upon the Buddha's teachings, we should refrain from making reckless remarks about them. A wise person would choose to do so.

March 29

Bear in Mind

YUKHOK CHOYING RANGDROL (1872–1952), a contemporary Tibetan, is widely recognized as a realized yogi of the Great Perfection. He usually assumed a wrathful appearance to train his disciples, making strict, high demands, and he rarely granted audiences, except for special cases. Our beloved lama, Jigme Phuntsok Rinpoche, had the good fortune to meet him at age fifteen.

During his later years, Choying Rangdrol built retreat huts on mountains near the Wengda area in Serthar, Sichuan Province, and taught a hundred retreatants. Many of his disciples attained realization and displayed various signs of accomplishment.

Once, his disciple Sonam Phuntsok requested that he bestow an incomparable instruction. The master taught:

> Visualize your supremely kind guru on the crown of your head. Pray constantly to receive the four empowerments. Merge your mind with the guru's wisdom. Perceive all appearances as the guru's body, all sounds as the guru's speech, and all discursive thoughts as the display of the guru's mind. In brief, all phenomena—animate or inanimate—are entirely the manifestation of the guru. While eating, visualize the guru at your throat and offer him the food as amrita. This offering will dispel defilements and transform ordinary food into *tsog* offerings. As you sleep, visualize the guru at the center of your heart, radiating light that reaches all realms. You

then melt into light and become one with the guru. When death approaches, do not become frightened or confused. Calm down. Imagine that your mind merges inseparably with the guru's wisdom and remains in that state, which is the essential transference of consciousness for the dying. Even if you were to study with me for a hundred years, I would not have any better teachings than these. Remember them well!

The master's teaching is precious, surpassing even the wish-granting jewel of the world. Anyone reading these words, the very embodiment of sublime wisdom, cannot but experience a refreshing insight. If this is not the case, that person may be suffering from heart stones.

March 31

Getting Transformed

WHEN TURNING the mind toward a spiritual journey, one makes a sharp turn in one's attitude and behavior. With the sword of wisdom, one can cut through the many knotty problems, impediments, and worries in the secular world.

The great Tibetan siddha Geshe Ben (Tsultrim Gyalwa) used to be a bandit who terrified local people with his rough and murderous ways. After seeing his own mistakes, he quickly broke from his outlaw life and took monastic ordination. Applying rigorous discipline and being watchful of his own faults, he eventually attained realization and bliss in his mind stream.

With diligent practice, a spiritual seeker will come to realize the truth of the universe and human life. As the Dharma seed sprouts in one's mind, the old perceptions bound by eight worldly concerns are shattered to pieces. All of a sudden, a wide vista opens, as boundless as the blue sky, allowing wisdom and compassion to expand and grow.

Even for someone with a deep-rooted attachment to secular affairs, all it takes is faith and perseverance to break free. Like a sharp iron shovel, the Buddha's teaching will invincibly slough off the mud of fame and fortune and uproot all worldly clinging.

As a spiritual practitioner, have I achieved any significant transformation yet?

April 3

Random Thoughts

QINGMING DAY is the traditional spring Memorial Day in Han China for paying homage to ancestors and fallen heroes. In a steady stream, many head to the outskirts of the city with fresh flowers, ready to sweep the tombs of their predecessors and martyrs.

There is a famous poem associated with this day:

> The rain drizzles down in a spray on spring Memorial Day,
> while mourners travel with hearts lost in sadness.
> When asked where to find a tavern to stop by,
> a shepherd boy points at a village amid apricot blossoms.

Yet I was alone, queuing for physical exams in a hospital. The demons of illness have been raging horrendous wars in my frail body, leaving me anxious and helpless. But whoever we may be, we must bear the miseries of being sick alone. Only in disease do we experience first-hand the sufferings of birth, sickness, aging, and death, which otherwise seem vague when we are healthy.

After waiting more than an hour at the billing department, finally it was my turn. It costs 260 yuan for a blood test alone. Seeing many patients wearing ragged clothes, I wondered how they could pay high medical fees. No wonder the saying goes: "If you are poor, try not to get sick. The threshold of the hospital is too high to cross." The only alternative for people unable to pay for medical care is to wait helplessly to die; it's miserable!

As I had to wait for the lab report, I sat under a ficus tree known to be 150 years old. I can't imagine that this tree is older than my great-grandfather. While my great-grandfather has been long gone, this tree still towers majestically. How amazing! Our human life span is no match for trees. Even if we manage to be disease free, our days are limited. Impermanence is indeed frightening!

On the ride home after getting my report, I saw a large building said to be owned by someone quite advanced in age. Musing over this older man nearing the end of his life and the big building that would remain strong after his departure, I felt sorry for those still making long-term plans. I was preoccupied with these random thoughts all morning instead of reading books or reciting scriptures, alas!

April 5
On the balcony, at noon on Qingming Day

Missionary Nun

UPON SEEING today's diary heading, some of you may wonder: As a Buddhist, why am I suddenly interested in the affairs of non-Buddhists? But the object of my admiration and respect today, the renowned Catholic nun Mother Teresa, is in my heart a living buddha or bodhisattva, beyond the simple definition of religious faith.

Mother Teresa was born into a well-educated Yugoslavian family and attended Catholic schools since childhood. At eighteen, she went to Calcutta, India, where she initially enjoyed a comfortable European lifestyle in a monastery with manicured gardens. However, discovering the utter misery of people outside the monastery walls shattered her peaceful and sheltered life. She could no longer turn a blind eye to the eyes that yearned for caring. Driven by a strong sense of purpose and against the fierce opposition of those around her, she ventured into the slums alone. Bravely, she carried on her slender back all the pains and sorrows of beings in the world. On her frail shoulders, she assumed the heavy burden of rescuing those in need from the slums.

There are many stories of her helping suffering, neglected, despised beings. A lonely older man was lying on a bed. No one cared for him or checked whether he was still breathing. The only visitor he ever expected was the Lord of Death. Instead, Mother Teresa walked into his room. A drunk was stretched out on the street, brutally beaten and severely injured, expecting nothing but indifference. Mother Teresa helped and escorted him to the House of the Pure Heart, founded by her. A tramp, lying curled up on the road, his body covered with oozing sores and maggots, received nothing but spiteful looks of disgust from passersby. Mother Teresa tenderly bound up his wounds and woeful heart, bringing comfort and warmth. Her footprints covered more than half the earth—Calcutta, Yemen, London, Melbourne, New York, and China. She founded more than a hundred charities to serve people experiencing poverty. She took in 61,273 abandoned babies in a period of merely six years.

Her untiring efforts finally gained the recognition of the world. In 1979 she was awarded the prestigious Nobel Peace Prize and became a household name overnight. She donated all her prize money to charities.

Although she was a Catholic nun, Mother Teresa had absolute respect for the religion of others. Every patient's funeral was held according to that person's religious faith. She touched the hearts of the world with her friendly, easygoing words and simple manner:

"There is a hunger for ordinary bread, and there is a hunger for love, for kindness, for thoughtfulness—this is the great poverty that makes people suffer so much."

"Although a tiny water droplet may not be worth mentioning, the gathering of a few droplets becomes a trickling rivulet, bringing some relief to those parched with thirst. "

"Although a single yarn is insignificant, the combination of several yarns can be used to weave cloth, bringing warmth to those shivering in the cold. "

"Although one grain of rice is hardly worth noticing, it is only by combining many grains of rice that there may be a bowl of porridge, bringing strength to those suffering from harsh starvation."

"We ourselves feel that what we are doing is just a drop in the ocean. But the ocean would be less because of that one missing drop."

"I do not agree with the big way of doing things. To us, what matters is the individual."

Let us follow Mother Teresa's example. With a humble and willing spirit, we will give up the ambition of accomplishing earthshaking deeds and start serving humanity bit by bit.

April 9

Distracted Mind

HERE IS ADVICE from Longchenpa that I sincerely appreciate. Although I have not been able to follow it specifically due to my obscurations, I'd love to share its golden wisdom here:

> On all occasions, be vigilant about your own mind. If distraction is unavoidable, perform prostrations or circumambulations that are applicable even in a distracting setting. At all times, stay away from evil deeds. If there is time for solitude, practice samadhi meditation and other exalted practices; do not waste your day being muddle-headed.

In other words, we should not let pointless diversions hijack our precious time. Ensure we are well-aligned with the Dharma under any circumstances and in any mood.

With vigilance, some individuals can keep up their practice even while living in a bustling city with many attractions and diversions. They find time to recite scriptures, meditate, or even practice dream yoga without outward displays. Gendun Chophel wrote:

> Being ever mindful amidst distractions
> and maintaining wakefulness in nightly sleep,
> a wise person progresses fast, like a prized steed,
> galloping far ahead of ordinary people.

The scholar Tao Yuanming of the Jin dynasty says in a poem:

> Amid lots of hustle and bustle I live,
> yet bothered not by sound nor fury.
> You ask me how this is possible—
> an unruffled mind makes a calm place.

Even if one's home is in the downtown area, noise and clamor from the street do not intrude. How could that be? It is because a peaceful mind will render its surroundings agreeable. Even within the world's hubbub, having a secluded mind naturally transports one to a secluded environment.

April 12

Some Reflections

TO RECEIVE proper treatment for my ailment and find a quiet place for translation work, I have lived in Xiamen for over one hundred days. It has been an easy and tranquil life for me—no massive office work to manage or packs of visitors to receive. It was not until a few days ago that I had to resume the title of khenpo after someone spotted me down the street.

An invitation was extended to me for lunch at the Nanputuo vegetarian restaurant. I accepted it readily, as I hadn't had visitors for a while and felt a little lonely. On my way there, I saw caged snakes and birds soon to be killed, and I ransomed them and set them free in the woods on the mountainside, making this trip worthwhile after all.

The restaurant had an elegant and serene decor, making one feel relaxed both physically and mentally. The chefs and attendants beamed with warm and sincere smiles, bringing out dishes embellished with colors and flavors to whet our appetites. The faces around the table looked peaceful and amicable, and the whole restaurant had an air of auspiciousness and harmony.

Sitting with us was a professor from Xiamen University. He said thoughtfully: "It is most important that we use *The Words of My Perfect Teacher* as a guide to building a strong foundation of spiritual study. If even luminary masters like Patrul Rinpoche received oral teachings and did the whole set of practices twenty-five times, what need to speak of ordinary people like us? I have read it five or six times by now, which helps me tremendously in subduing my negative emotions and dealing with the difficulties of daily life. In the past, unaware of the graduated path, I always salivated at receiving empowerment or doing so-called profound practices while entrapped in endless discursive thoughts. It dawns on me only now that there are no higher teachings than this book. If one faithfully follows its steps, the achievement will come for certain."

Hearing what he had to say, I felt delighted. My joy did not come from his profuse praise of me but rather from the fact that a Han Chinese was keen on *The Words of My Perfect Teacher*, even though he had not personally been to Larung Buddhist Academy. His astute and profound insight was quite unusual. In Tibetan monasteries, *The Words of My Perfect Teacher* is a high-priority course in the annual curriculum. It's worth rejoicing that such a tradition is taking root in Han China. This scholar seems to have profound worldly knowledge and a fine grasp of spiritual wisdom.

April 14

About Wars

L ACKING WISDOM, some people wishing to attain peace and
happiness think they can do so by waging war. Yet numerous
harsh lessons from time immemorial prove the absurdity of this notion.

For those unaffected by the trauma, wars are abstract news reports
or entertaining television dramas. But those who have suffered personally from the miseries of war will shudder at any recollection of it. And
people who have strong compassion will also experience intense pain
when thinking of war. War inflicts ordeals beyond healing in the hearts
of many people; war damages beautiful landscapes until unrepairable;
war smears blood over the white sheets of history's chapters. Because
of war, innocent people endure long-term violence and chaos, suffering tremendous pain. Millions have been forced to leave their homes,
becoming destitute; countless families have crumbled and loved ones
have been scattered far away. All this is to satisfy some people's craving to plunder resources, compete for territory, and seize power. Some
fools even contrive to make big bucks through war dealings, totally
ignorant of the dire consequences that will soon befall them.

All kinds of conflicts, from major wars between countries to trivial arguments among family members, result from lacking wisdom. As
spiritual practitioners, we must not wage wars but pray for peace for
the world, families, and our minds.

April 18

Lotus Pond

RIGHT IN FRONT of the Minnan Buddhist Academy main hall is a large pond where lotus flowers blossom one after the other in late spring. When the sun shines after a shower, crystalline water droplets roll on the leaves and blossoms, reflecting distinctive colors and charming the eyes. Verdant lotus leaves, ever elegant and poised, infuse the pond with exuberant vigor. Dragonflies and birds glide smoothly over the pond, taking in the flowers' fragrance to their hearts' delight. Fish ransomed from knives are now swimming at will in the pond, chit-chatting with the flowers about the marvel of freedom. The trees around the bank are bedecked with tender green baby buds, as if composing a movement to welcome the returning swallows. Monks promenade leisurely and meditatively. Does the revelation, "And lo! Here on the sprig is spring in its fullness," click in their hearts?

Is this intoxicating spring scenery the manifestation of the Buddha and bodhisattvas? As I immerse myself fully in it, not only do I feel refreshed mentally and physically, but I am also inspired to realize the profundity of this Zen poem:

> Bamboos, all green and vibrant, are nothing but a display of wisdom.
> Flowers, all yellow and lush, are entirely the expression of Dharmakaya.

Monks of the Minnan Buddhist Academy have designed this lotus pond thoughtfully. A wall built around the pond deflects the noise and busyness of the city and carves out a quiet space for practitioners. No wonder that even students from neighboring Xiamen University like to come over to enjoy the solitude of the monastery while doing their homework.

A set of poetic couplets came to my mind:

> The sounds of wind, water, insects, birds, chanting, and the
>   gongs of 365 days—all sounds are but silence.
> The moon, mountains, grass blades, trees, sunsets, and the
>   48,000 rolling hills and terrain—all forms are but emptiness.

If posted inside the main hall, these couplets may inspire some readers.

Doing spiritual practice in such a setting is quite a blessing. I wish we could have a lotus pond like this at Larung Gar!

April 19
By the Lotus Pond

Beautiful Singing

A LONG TIME AGO, there was a ravishingly beautiful dancer named Incomparable Lady. Her dances were fluid and graceful, her singing voice pristine as celestial music, which brought tremendous delight to many. The lyrics of one of her songs especially evoked deep contemplation in listeners:

> With the mind abiding in the Dharma always,
> one will not engage in non-virtue and fall into the lower
>   realms.
> With the bright light shining, darkness vanishes—
> what a shame if one still wanders onto the wrong path!

Hearing this song, those with distracted minds found themselves deep in thought. The ministers plotting to end the king's life subdued their malicious intention. The ascetic monk who wished to resume secular life dropped his plan. Those tormented by afflictive emotions became free from them. Thus, through her melodic singing, practically everyone—from king to everyday citizens—was suffused with incomparable bliss.

All this is not a fabrication but a true story. People then had fewer karmic defilements; even simple lyrics could awaken them. However, today the masses are obsessed with meaningless things and with rave songs and dances that incite their desires. Spiritual teachings, even the exalted essential instructions, are met with deaf ears or regarded like worn-out shoes. How times have changed!

Ancient songs and melodies are rich in spiritual nourishment, and to dig in and extract the nectar from them is what a wise person would do. Some teachings may seem easy and plain; please do not take them lightly. Even merely one verse, if pondered profoundly and practiced earnestly, would have the power to uproot afflictive emotions.

April 21

The Summit

THE PASSAGE of human life is rough and bumpy; the path to liberation is winding and rugged. A coward, dreading difficulties, never dares to look up at the towering mountain. A hero, armored with diligence, charges courageously toward the summit of spiritual attainment.

People from various places all gather at this mountain slope. They pick their path according to their inclination. Only the one who scales the summit is the real champion. With unshakable determination and indomitable courage, the warriors will not shrink when facing obstacles on the road nor shrivel by sheer cliffs, overhanging rocks, or thistles. Without hesitation, they persistently and unwaveringly tread the path straight on. Eventually, they reach the summit of their deepest aspirations. There, breathtaking vistas are at their feet, and all distant mountains appear to shrink before their eyes.

While climbing, some (those with wrong views) may get lost and stray into the deep woods; some (those with failing faith) may lose confidence and turn back to the starting point; some (the Theravada practitioners) could stall halfway due to fatigue and inactivity; some (those seeking worldly gains) may be lured by picturesque scenery and take a detour; and still some (Vajrayana practitioners) will just take the trolley and arrive at the destination with ease.

A boundless view is found only at the perilous peak. However, this summit is reserved only for the undaunted and the courageous, never for the timid, faithless, and lazy ones.

April 22
At Wulao Peak, Xiamen

Loquat Fruit

DUE TO the El Niño effect, the spring weather is very hot and humid, almost like midsummer. On the street, I caught sight of a vendor carrying a basketful of golden fruit embellished with green leaves. The fruit looked juicy and fresh, making one's mouth water. I had never seen anything like it and learned they are called loquats. I peeled one open and put it in my mouth. A refreshing and delicious juice filled my mouth—yum! Such tasty fruit must be the treat of the god realm! After a bit of bargaining, I brought dozens at a steep price and hurried home, thinking to savor them with my readings.

Turning the pages of the *Great Biography of Shakyamuni Buddha, the White Lotus*, I read this: "How many people in the world will enjoy everlasting happiness? How many people in the world will suffer endless miseries? How many have never experienced suffering? After attaining happiness, how many have enjoyed it forever?" Indeed, there will be happiness throughout life's journey, but suffering will also be there. No matter who you are, one is bound to taste the assorted bittersweetness of life. A person of wisdom, therefore, must meet life's ups and downs calmly—neither becoming arrogant with success nor discouraged by failure.

The ancient Chinese *Tao Te Ching* also states:

> Good fortune follows upon disaster; disaster lurks within good fortune.

Luck and misfortune come in turn. All things are relative, and everything is impermanent. Therefore, when there is an intense emotion of pleasure or pain, we should look straight at its essence. This is a crucial and decisive way to practice in a happy or sad moment.

While engrossed in these thoughts, I completely forgot my plan to enjoy the loquats. Yet I tasted something more delicious from reading than eating the exotic fruit. The sage's teaching is the most delectable loquat in the world; it will never rot and is ready to be savored even a hundred or a thousand years later.

April 23

Question and Answer

A MINNAN BUDDHIST Academy teacher asked me today: "Does the Buddha still perceive sentient beings after having attained buddhahood?" This is a question many Buddhists often raise. Some say: "An enlightened buddha has eliminated all conceptions of self and other beings; therefore, he'll not perceive sentient beings." Still, others wonder: "How can the Buddha tame sentient beings if he does not see them?"

The answer to these questions is as follows: To the enlightened Buddha, in his wisdom that knows the nature of things as it is, all phenomena are in a state of equality; the Buddha never entertains the thought of a self, a being, a living creature, or an individual. In his wisdom that perceives all possibly existing phenomena, the Buddha knows every thought of and everything about all sentient beings without confusion or clinging.

This teaching from Rongzom Pandita offers an example: There are two persons in a room. The first person is dreaming, while the second one, who has the psychic power of knowing other's minds, is awake. The second person sees the first person's dream without clinging because he knows it is a dream. Should the dreamer have nightmares and suffer tremendously, the second person, through his miraculous power, can enter the dream and dispel the horror until the dreamer wakes up. In the same way, the Buddha knows sentient beings' conceptual thoughts and their perceived phenomena. The Buddha has no attachment and, with skillful means suiting each individual, leads all beings gradually onto the path of liberation.

Master Dharmakirti says: "The wisdom of the Tathagata is inconceivable." Indeed, even bhumi-level bodhisattvas cannot thoroughly fathom the wisdom and qualities of the Tathagata, not to mention ordinary beings. Before we can comprehend the ultimate wisdom of the Buddha, we shall first establish robust faith and rely on scriptural authority.

April 24

Massage Treatment

I FOLLOW MY doctor's advice to get massage treatment daily. As we see each other every day, the masseur and I have become well acquainted. He is pretty deft in his work and is also a good conversationalist. Soon after I lay down, he let out a flood of words: "You Buddhists always talk about karmic retribution. Karma is something we'd better believe in. My next-door neighbor was impious to his parents, so his wife ran off with someone else. I was born blind in this life, so I must have committed some evil actions in my past. On the other hand, I also must have done some good deeds because I was able to learn my trade and support myself."

I pondered his words for a while and realized that many non-disabled people often cannot do as well as or better than a blind person. They are ignorant of the principle of cause and effect and indulge in hostile actions. When encountering misfortune, they only resent their fate and blame others. They do not reckon with the following adage:

> If you want to know what you have done in your past lives,
> just observe what this life of yours has been like.
> If you want to know how your future lives are likely to be,
> just observe what you have been doing in this life.

All our fate, good or bad, results from our deeds. If everyone had faith in causality, as my masseur does, the world would have one measure more of decency and less hostility.

While deep in thought, suddenly I felt a heavy blow on my back that made me cry out with pain: "Ouch! Do spare your brute force!"

The masseur apologized quickly: "I overdid it. I am sorry!"

I said: "In Tibetan Buddhism, there is a great master called Mipham Rinpoche. He once said, 'Even if the whole world is full of evil beings, one should still maintain one's noble conduct.' Although you are not a Buddhist, this saying will benefit you. You should always be like the lotus flower, which emerges from the mud without being sullied."

He replied: "Thank you so much for your advice. I shall follow it faithfully."

Well, the heavy pounding landing on me today may well be the result of my karma, but if this episode can bring my masseur some understanding of the truth, my pain is all worthwhile.

April 25

Nice Chatting

A SMALL HILL called Wulao Peak rises behind Minnan Buddhist Academy. Though it lacks the imposing height of the Tibetan mountains, it is a lovely spot to hike and enjoy a panoramic view of the surrounding area. Climbing to its peak and seeing the entire Xiamen City spread below one's feet, the saying "a view from the top of Wulao dwarfs Fujian Province" instantly comes to mind.

This hill has lush forests, green grass, twittering birds, and chirping insects. It's an inviting place to do spiritual meditation. Halfway up the hilltop is Arinya Place, a sanctuary visited often by local residents. It is also where the Dharma teacher Jiqun and I planned to meet up. Master Jiqun has long endeavored to spread the Buddhadharma and is well-respected in Buddhist circles for his accomplishment. He has trained many monks, nuns, and lay professionals who now carry out Dharma activities in many places. It's an immense pleasure to meet and talk to him.

Sipping Kungfu tea, the beverage of the Min people, we exchanged thoughts and experiences. I mentioned the traditions of Tibetan Buddhism, how it follows spiritual mentors and the many heartrending stories of past great masters. We paused to admire some of the most inspiring ones. I also stated that listening to, reflecting on, and meditating on the teachings is central, and none is dispensable. He agreed, sighing that, indeed, in this time of five degenerations, people must work on the three wisdom tools to establish the correct view and uproot afflictive emotions. Hearing his words, I felt like Boya meeting his soul mate Ziqi. The purpose of Buddhism is to empower people to overcome confused emotions. Unless the Buddha's teachings are infused into one's mind and applied to daily activities, all other feats, such as building temples and erecting statues, are superficial and meaningless. Regrettably, only a few people grasp this truth.

Without us noticing it, the sun was setting in the west. It's time for me to leave, with the wish for another heart-to-heart talk while we are still around. But as impermanence pervades all places, I fear this wish may not come true!

April 26

Pith Instruction

JIGME TENPAI NYIMA of Pema, Qinghai, was the leading disciple of the great Ju Mipham Rinpoche. He could give brilliant teachings on *The Way of the Bodhisattva* when he was barely eight. On such occasions, he often held a text holder almost the same height as his body (traditional Tibetan text holders, made of silk brocade reinforced with bamboo, are about 2 feet long). Even seasoned yogis would marvel at such a sight and lavish him with praise. Patrul Rinpoche was pleased to comment: "Now that Thondup Rinpoche (another name for Jigme Tenpai Nyima) teaches the Dharma at the age of eight, it shows that the Nyingma tradition is rising high and the future is bright!"

Jigme Tenpai Nyima left many poems and jewel-like teachings for future generations on the Great Perfection and the *Great Web of Magical Illusion*. Today I pick one passage from them to share: "The naturally occurring timeless awareness is hard to grasp by people inclined to intellectual speculation and analysis; only through constantly praying to the lama with sheer devotion and faith, coupled with diligent practice, can we see the true face of the mind. As we get better, we can maintain this recognition of the mind even when reading scriptures such as the *Seven Treasures*. Our insight and the wisdom of discernment will gradually increase, bringing us enormous benefit."

Therefore, observing your mind while reading books or reading books while chanting mantras is fantastic. Such multitasking may prove difficult for a beginner, but mastering it is a matter of time. Many khenpos at Larung have become adepts, and that's how they manage to accumulate an astonishing number of mantra recitations over the years.

Nonetheless, there are people with high opinions of themselves who neither bother to read books nor recite mantras. They waste their precious lives on futile activities and do not deserve to be called practitioners!

April 28

Heart Treasure

IN WORLDLY POSSESSIONS, Nyingma masters might not leave much to their heirs compared with wealthy tycoons. Instead, they have stashed away dazzling jewels of sublimated wisdom and compassion in treasure troves unmatchable by any mundane inheritance. Anyone equipped with the key of faith will find in these vaults gems that will bring boundless joy.

Today, I made a treasure-hunting trip to Lhala Chodri Rinpoche's chamber. I found it filled to the brim with innumerable gems that made the greedy me ecstatic to no end. But with my limited strength, I could not carry them all out and only picked out one passage on recognizing the nature of the mind. With an urge to share, here I am presenting my translation for dear Dharma friends to enjoy. However, those without the Great Perfection transmission should refrain from reading it—otherwise, a reprimand from the Dharma Protectors will surely come.

Briefly, here is a direct pointing-out instruction on the heart's essence:

All phenomena appear because of the mind. When one investigates the mind that is having a thought, nothing, such as shapes or colors, can be identified. The so-called beginningless mind is only a conceptual imputation. A thorough investigation of the "I" and "my mind" yields only emptiness with nothing substantial beyond that; this is the view of Madhyamaka. When no longer searching around, the mind naturally rests in emptiness with the unceasing display of phenomena. Such a state of self-cognizance that is naturally lucid is the realm of Great Perfection.

Thus, one remains undistracted by external circumstances, unsullied by subtle discursive thoughts, and rests in a vividly clear and awake state.

It's crucial to train the mind continuously in this way, like a mighty, unceasing river. Besides this, one must also exert oneself in supportive activities such as taking refuge, generating bodhichitta, practicing guru yoga, observing worldly virtues, and abandoning evil.

I, the old yogi of Nyingmapa, Sonam Khyentse [Lhala Chodri Rinpoche], have no other daily practices besides these. May beings with good karma also come to know this heart treasure!

Aren't we fortunate to meet with this precious heart treasure? Let's cherish it dearly! However, some people think they already have the requisite faculties for Great Perfection. Deeming taking refuge, doing guru yoga, arousing bodhichitta, adopting worldly virtues, and abandoning evil as practices for dull people, they ignore them and don't bother to practice. Do they imagine their aptitude surpasses that of our lineage masters?

The heart treasures handed down from past masters are now fully revealed to us. We should reflect upon them deeply, word by word, and meld them into our mind streams. Then, having recognized the nature of the mind, we continue the meditation for a long time. Only by doing so can we prove ourselves worthy of the blessings from our masters and the Three Jewels.

April 29

Project Completed

I FEEL TODAY deserves commemoration because a significant endeavor of my life—the translation of the *Great Biography of Shakyamuni Buddha, the White Lotus*—has just been completed. I started this task on December 25, 2001. On that day, people in Xiamen celebrated Christmas in various ways. I comforted myself by taking the festive scene outside as cheers for the foundation-laying ceremony of my translation project.

Buddha Shakyamuni, the founder of Buddhism, performed innumerable activities of the Six Transcendent Perfections from his initial aspiration to final enlightenment. His deeds are incredibly moving stories that touch me deeply every time I read them, and I was inspired to translate this biography so that others can appreciate it too. Today I am glad to see my aspiration is finally fulfilled.

The launch of my translation last year also coincided with building a highrise across from my residence. Its groundbreaking ceremony was adorned with colorful banners and attended by throngs of cheering crowds. Reportedly, the building started with a costly blueprint and its construction mobilized hundreds of workers with modern engineering tools. Compared with their grand style, my translation project seems overly humble. I have neither a vast workforce nor hefty support funds, only a proofreader of the typescript. Nonetheless, we do have an unshakable faith in the Buddha that outshines mundane pursuits, which alone is enough to elevate us to the rank of indomitable nobles in spirit.

After more than one hundred working days, the highrise is in the final stage of construction and will soon be ready for owner occupancy. My project, likewise, has reached the finishing line. While the developers must feel good about their noteworthy accomplishments, I also feel proud of my contribution, which is more meaningful. A few hundred years from now, buildings made from cement, brick, and tiles will be gone with no trace left behind. In stark contrast to this impermanence, the spiritual legacy of the Buddha will remain. Unaffected by the confines of time and space, it will arouse faith in readers across continents and generations, leading them steadily onto the path of liberation.

The best inheritance to leave for future generations is not an impressive building, gold, silver, or jewels, but a towering spiritual mansion that protects the mind from the thunderstorms of delusion.

May 3

May Fourth

TODAY IS Youth Day in China, commemorating the May Fourth Movement that shook the nation in 1919. As time passes, however, young people no longer emphasize fighting feudalism or oppression but instead celebrate the day in various ways.

As for me, I found myself in the company of young people on an outing to release captive animals. Three ships loaded with sea creatures whose lives were once at grave stake sailed off the coast in an impressive formation. The two hundred participants included local Buddhists from Xiamen, monks and nuns from nearby monasteries and Buddhist academies, and laity from Fuzhou, Taiwan, and Hong Kong. Against the blue sea, the maroon-and-yellow monastic robes and the householders' varicolored attire stood out vividly and brightly. It was quite a marvelous sight to behold.

During my four-month stay in this coastal city, at lunch or dinner time, the stench of seafood wafted through the open window, polluting the fresh air of the shore and making me and my friend, also from Tibet, lose our appetites. We have long wished to save the poor fish, crustaceans, and so forth from meeting their end at the knife, but it is only today that we are fulfilling our wish. Even though the number of lives we save can't compare to those killed in the city, we are still grateful for the opportunity.

Once, a county magistrate named Pan Gong forbade his subjects from catching live fish by instigating severe punishments for perpetrators. Years later, when he was about to leave his official post, a wailing sound as distressed as at the loss of one's parents was heard from the waters, filling people's hearts with sadness and amazement. I often pray that such a benevolent county magistrate will appear again in Xiamen, thus saving many beings from being killed. Nonetheless, the practice of lifesaving is well established here, I was told, primarily due to the free distribution of ten thousand booklets of *The Merit of Releasing Live Beings* by an aspiring layperson. The tradition has thus gradually flourished down to this day.

Today's lifesaving activity is reportedly the largest in recent years in this area. Whether the scale of activity is large or small, we have taken a stand against oppression on behalf of these sea creatures. The value of good deeds depends not so much on their scale as on consistency. When virtue is practiced daily and enhanced monthly, we hope that the tragedy of taking other beings' lives will no longer exist one hundred years from now.

May 4

At Ease

PEOPLE living in the world—be they nobles or commoners, rich or poor, powerful or lowly—are all subject to mood swings of happiness and sadness unless they have attained the ultimate realization. All mental afflictions—remorse, fatigue, pain, hatred, and apathy—can pop up for no reason. Then suddenly, the whole world seems to be arrayed against oneself. At other times, one may feel blissful, upbeat, energetic, joyful, and carefree—as if even the sun exists solely for one's sake. In this way, anyone incapable of taking the helm of the mood will be at the mercy of the rollercoaster torture of bitterness and sweetness.

As spiritual seekers, we should recognize that all these moods are the phantom displays of our confused minds. It is said: "Calmness and peace are the nature of things; busyness and disorder are the fabrications of humans." When confronted with the ups and downs of the world, we shall stay imperturbable and save ourselves from extreme mood swings.

At Larung Academy, Khenpo Losang Chophel is an outstanding example in this respect. The furnishings at his place have remained almost the same for over ten years. His prayer wheels, scriptures, statues, portable furnace, and a few articles for everyday use are arranged neatly and nicely, which please the eyes and calm the mind. He often sits up straight on the bed, either reading or practicing. In whichever way the turbulent world changes around him, he is ready to face it with equanimity.

What about a person like me? Soon after I arrived at Larung, I borrowed a place, then I built a straw house, a sawmill slab house, and finally a two-room house of wood. I spent a lot of energy on these frivolous jobs. Burdened by the task of providing my lump of flesh with temporary lodgings, I kept on making remodeling plans. I often asked myself: When will I learn to be content with a small cottage where I sit on the bed and immerse myself in the Dharma?

People busy themselves incessantly. Today it is singing songs with someone dressed in a white tunic; tomorrow, dancing with someone in a black jacket; and the day after, hitting the bar with someone in a red dress. For Dharma persons, today it is joining a Zen meditation; tomorrow, chanting Buddha Amitabha's holy name; and the day after, receiving Great Perfection empowerment. Although they proclaim such dabbling combines the three approaches of Zen, Pure Land, and the Secret Mantra in one, they accomplish nothing.

A genuinely spiritual person sees the world's vanity as transient as a fleeting cloud. A verse in *The Roots of Wisdom* says:

> Unmoved by gaining or losing a favor,
> I casually watch the blooming and fading of flowers in the
>   garden.
> Unconcerned about holding or leaving a post,
> I remain as carefree as the clouds rolling and dispersing in
>   the sky.

Shouldn't we aspire to attain such a state of mind?

May 6

Lotus Root

M Y FRIEND bought several lotus roots and left them on the table. These whitish roots looked tender and inviting. To satisfy my curiosity, my friend told me how lotus root is grown and used. Thus I learned that lotus root has remarkable value according to traditional Chinese medicine. When eaten raw, it clears heat and nourishes the lungs, cools the blood, and promotes circulation. When eaten cooked, it tones the spleen and stimulates the appetite. It is antidiarrheal as well as blood-enriching, mood-calming, and brain-invigorating. Finally, it can promote a long and healthy life. Confucius says: "In a party of three, there must be one I can learn from." I am blessed to be in the company of such a knowledgeable friend.

The lotus root grows in the mud but remains white. Its stem is hollow and straight, having no lateral branches or tendrils. The open center signifies the virtue of humility; its straightness symbolizes upright and firm character; its lack of lateral stems and tendrils illustrates it has no discursive thoughts or outward clinging. The root has been appreciated since ancient times and is very popular among famous personages. The poet Hanyu praised it this way: "Cool as frost and sweet as honey. Imbibe one piece, and all ailments are gone." In his *Ode to Imperial Garden*, Sima Xiangru of the Han dynasty writes: "Flocks of water birds alight on the surface of the river and drift gently with the tide. Some other birds perch on the sandy islets thick with weeds. They twitter and chirp while pecking at algae and water grass, or enjoy chewing water chestnuts and lotus roots."

In addition, the lotus root was the food that sustained many ancient practitioners through their austere disciplines. *The Great Biography of Shakyamuni Buddha, the White Lotus* tells us that when the Buddha was a Brahmin ascetic practicing in the mountains, his primary source of sustenance was the lotus root.

Indeed, the lotus root is a fantastic plant endowed with beneficial power. Eating it nourishes our body; emulating its essence uplifts our spirit. What other food is superior to it, conferring two benefits in one? From now on, I shall eat more lotus root, as it is a nourishment blessed by the Buddha.

May 7

Keep Going

FROM EARLY YOUTH to adulthood, the person I admired most was Lama Yiluo. He was a man of solid build whose hand perpetually moved the mala beads and whose mouth constantly recited mantras. On his face was a scar left by robbers he encountered in his youth when he went to Lhasa on foot. Instead of being a blemish, this facial mark made him even more likable.

I took room and board at his house when I attended elementary school. Every day before dawn, he would get up and start doing prostrations. At the same time, he would recite prayers. After breakfast, he read books and reviewed his daily Dharma sadhanas. He sat in meditation in the afternoon and recited scriptures in the evening. For over ten years, he kept the same schedule repeatedly without interruption.

At that time, I took it for granted that all practitioners behaved as he did and felt there was nothing special about him. But now I see that I and others only engage our practices in fits and starts. We get serious only when we are in good spirits, but when our mood falls, we become distracted and lag in practice. This glaring contrast makes his perseverance all the more admirable.

At the time of his passing at age eighty-seven, he had accumulated 500 million mantras, an astonishing number. Comparing my meager diligence with his, I feel ashamed.

The *Mahayana Abhidharma Sangiti Shastra* says: "Practitioners on the path of accumulation should endeavor in studying, contemplating, and meditating on the Dharma. To tame the six senses, eat appropriately and avoid sleeping in the early or late part of the night (that is, sleep only in the middle section)."

> Without adding up many little steps, a journey of a thousand
>   miles cannot be accomplished.
> Without the pouring together of many tiny streams, there will
>   be no big oceans.

On-and-off diligence amounts to nothing; only persistence over a life-time is what counts.

May 8
Written on a lovely spring morning

Air Disaster

I HAVE SPENT A carefree and noteworthy four months in Xiamen. Thanks to the pleasant environment this city provided for me and my friend—fine scenery and superb weather, for instance—I finished my translation of *The Great Biography of Shakyamuni Buddha, the White Lotus*. Now it's time for me to reluctantly say goodbye to Kulangsu, with its coconut-grove breeze, and bid farewell to the tranquil setting of Wulao Peak. Today, I am returning to Chengdu, leaving Xiamen behind.

Two days ago, an airplane flying from Beijing to Dalian crashed into the sea near Dalian. Over one hundred people perished—old and young, male and female. This news shook the world and made me and those around me uneasy. The airport appeared unusually deserted because many passengers canceled their flights to outsmart their fate. Those who boarded the airplane seemed anxious, as if they just realized that their lives were at the mercy of the Lord of Death. In reality, human life is highly fragile, and Death always hangs over our heads, whether on the ground or in the air. A bouncing, vibrant being can be instantly shattered into many pieces.

The scripture says:

> Human beings, young or old, wise or foolish,
> all are perpetually marching forward
> into the domain of formidable Death—
> each will breathe their last.

In the air, at sea, or in the valley,
nowhere is there a safe place to hide,
as there is nowhere Death does not butt in.

The victims of this disaster came from different countries and varied in age and gender. All had been living their own lives until they met the same doom and died simultaneously in the air over the Pacific Ocean. It seems, sadly, that there is no guarantee of anything pacific above the Pacific Ocean.

As the great departure approaches, even if you own all the wealth of Jambudvipa (the southern continent where humans live), you can't bribe the minions of Death. Even if you seal yourself inside an impenetrable chamber protected by hundreds of thousands of strong guards, you can't escape the claws of Death.

Most people can do nothing but feel utterly hopeless on the deathbed. Shouldn't we, living on borrowed time, seriously prepare ourselves for the inevitable last moment?

May 9

True Happiness

WHAT IS true happiness? People have diverse answers to this question. To those who love money, being rich is true happiness; to those who desire glory, becoming famous is true happiness; to those who seek intimacy, finding love is true happiness; to a wise person, pursuing a spiritual path is true happiness. Indeed, these kaleidoscopic definitions show that everyone has their own interpretation of happiness.

Yet upon closer examination, those who run after worldly fame and pleasure will never experience true happiness. Mipham Rinpoche says: "A person whose mind is pounded by the waves of discursive thoughts will never experience happiness in practice."

A Tibetan Rinpoche admonished his Western students: "The wealth and abundance you Westerners enjoy rival those of the celestial realm. But you are sleeping on a bed of thorns; no matter how you toss about, you can't get comfortable. Until you are free from negative emotions, happiness will always elude you."

So-called happiness in the mundane world is nothing but the cause of samsaric suffering. The stronger you grasp illusory pleasures, the tighter you are ensnared in the swirl of samsara. One will enjoy everlasting, true happiness only when letting go of self-grasping completely!

May 12

Hidden Treasures

AT THE MENTION of hidden treasures—*terma*—most Buddhists immediately assume that it is special to the Nyingma lineage of Tibetan Buddhism. But to hold such a viewpoint is a sign of being ill-informed.

In the *Sutra of Abiding in Samadhi*, the Buddha says: "As I pass into nirvana, my body relics and the Dharma will remain in the world. Having meditated on the doctrines, buddhas and bodhisattvas will codify and store them in treasure chests, conceal them inside stupas, under the earth, or in the rocks—bidding gods, nagas, and demigods to protect them. These Dharma treasures are as indestructible as the pure precepts. In the future at the destined time, great masters of different lineages, cued by the buddhas and bodhisattvas, will reveal the treasures, decipher them, and benefit all sentient beings." The *Sutra of Practicing the Authentic Dharma* also says: "Ananda, those who codify Dharma teachings and conceal them so that fresh, unimpaired Dharma will long remain in this world are making superb offerings. They will obtain four benefits. What are these four? They are: attaining the buddha-eyes, and . . . " Obviously, the Buddha has clearly described the origin of terma; our misunderstanding comes from reading too few scriptures.

Regardless, the benefits of terma in this degenerate time are unfathomable. One of the great revealers, Terton Pema Lingpa, says: "Terma—the profound, complete, faultless, and immense treasure—will guide numerous beings in degenerate times. Whoever has faith in terma now must have previously met the Great Master of Oddiyana,

Guru Rinpoche, and made pledges in front of him. Rejoice in your good fortune and strive to practice terma teachings, always remembering impermanence and awakening your buddha nature. You can be sure of attaining liberation in this very life!"

Regarding the merits, principles, debates, and questions of terma, there is detailed information in *The Comprehensive History of Terma* by Pema Lingpa. Those who are interested may wish to read it.

May 14

Golden Advice

TO REQUEST an audience with H. H. Jigme Phuntsok Rinpoche, Khenpo Gendun from Hongyuan made a special trip of several hundred kilometers to Chengdu, despite his old age. When I heard this, I quickly visited him at his hotel. Khenpo stays in a humble room furnished only with two old wooden beds and a wobbly table that seems about to fall apart. Yet he beamed as if he were in the heavenly realm. Although he is over seventy years old and has difficulty walking, he is still hale and hearty, his glowing, rosy cheeks exuding energy.

When Khenpo was at Larung Gar, I received teachings from him on thirteen major commentaries, such as the *Uttaratantra Shastra* and *Adornment of the Middle Way*. I owe him so much for his kindness and tutelage, and I will never forget the image of his diminutive figure holding the long, narrow texts.

When Khenpo was young, his thirst for Dharma drove him to many places to receive teachings from great masters, and he became well-versed in the sutra and tantra scriptures and commentaries. But he never thought he had learned enough and always continued to study. At Larung, he lived not far from my wooden cottage. When I happened to wake up at two or three in the morning, there would already be a dim light coming from his place. At times I'd sneak up to look and could see him diligently concentrating on reading and studying. One year, when our beloved Guru Jigme Phuntsok Rinpoche returned from Xinlong, the whole Larung Valley was filled with excited well-wishers and bustling activities. Still, all the hustle and bustle did not distract him from immersing himself deeply in the ocean of scriptures, which made him even more remarkable and outstanding. His conduct made a strong impression on me, and I took him as a role model and would not give in to laziness.

On this day, we have a heart-to-heart talk for quite a while. He looks at me with such tender and loving eyes that I feel a surge of warmth swelling up in me. He says he is now faking sickness and shutting his eyes to all external affairs. Leading a quiet life at his place, he devotes himself wholly to mantra recitation. His attendant tells me that since finishing teaching the Nyingma tradition at Beijing Buddhist College last year, just up until a few days ago, his master has been in a completely silent retreat with this sign posted on the door: "I am seriously ill. No visitors, please." They are returning to the mountain hermitage tomorrow and will start the retreat again the day after arriving. I don't know what he is practicing, but my guess is the supreme Great Perfection.

How extraordinary and desirable is his current situation! As for me now, I still cannot but subject myself to external circumstances. Deep in my heart, I yearn for places of solitude, even when living in the city; I long for total silence, though I have to talk nonsense. I yearn for unwavering awareness, though my mind always rushes here and there. Will my wishes ever be realized?

This is the path to follow—to study a great deal when we have the energy and to practice thoroughly once the Dharma has penetrated the heart, just like him. If we keep following the discursive thoughts of superficial virtue, when can we rest in the nature of the mind?

May 16

Love Arrow

A TIBETAN PROVERB SAYS: "An arrow lodged in the earth is easy to pull out, while a love arrow hit in the heart is by no means easy to remove." Love and lust are sharp arrows that bring suffering. The Buddha says in the *Dhammapada*: "The arrow you made may return to hurt you. The same goes with the inner arrow in the heart; love arrows bring suffering to beings."

No wonder Cupid, the Western god of love, is imaged as a winged boy wielding a bow and arrow, with which he wounds his victims. Although glorified in many poignant writings, poems, and lyrics, love is like an arrow: its nature is to harm. The *Dhammapada* says:

> From affection springs grief; from affection springs fear.
> For one who is wholly free from affection, there is no grief,
> so where is fear?

Love and lust are the causes of pain and suffering. If we were not weighed down by strong emotions of love, we would not have taken rebirth in samsara again and again. Separation from loved ones is indeed an unbearable sorrow. But lovers who never separate for a single day are not immune to tremendous anguish in their mutual attachment. Like a gorgeous sunset, beauty fades in no time; like a running brook, music is gone in a snap of the fingers; like the morning dew, worldly love evaporates in a blink. To fall in love intensely without knowing how to extricate oneself will only add layer upon layer of anguish.

How can we be free from it all? The answer is in a story told by the Buddha: A king was offered an elephant meticulously tamed by an elephant specialist. One day the trainer led an excursion into the forest with the king sitting on the elephant. Suddenly, upon sniffing the scent of a female elephant, the king's elephant became crazed and ran wildly to the horrified alarm of the king. Later the king severely admonished the trainer. The trainer replied: "When lust flares up, no lasso nor iron hook will work. As a trainer, I can only tame the elephant's body, not its mind. Only the Buddha can tame such beings' body and mind!"

Indeed, relying on the Buddha is the only way to save us from drowning in the torrents of love or being entangled in secular relationships. To fall into the terrific river of love and lust is to drift around in samsara. The *Surangama Sutra* says: "Until the river of lust and love dries up, there is no liberation." The only recourse is to practice the Buddha's teachings to run away from the flood of lust, dodge the love arrow, and be relieved from sorrow and fear.

The preeminent scholar Su Shi writes poetically: "To pacify the pounding waves of the suffering ocean, first let its feeder stream of love and lust run dry." To be rescued from the ocean of samsaric suffering, sentient beings must first cut the Gordian knot of all-consuming love.

In life's journey, how many people have not suffered from the painful arrow of love?

May 17

Dance Performance

AT THIS STAGE of human life, everyone is a dancer. Some performances are thrillingly spectacular, gripping everyone's attention, while others are bland, flat, and dull. If asked to name the most elegant and graceful dance, worldly and spiritual people have distinct ideas.

During the day, people hurry and busily rove about, killing time in endless idle gossip; at night, they drift to sleep, bleary-eyed. What portion of the day, if any, is committed to spiritual practice? If we get up one hour earlier and go to bed one hour later every day, we will save sixty hours in merely a month. A dancer wishing to perfect elegant dance moves would commit to persistent and painstaking daily practice; how can spiritual practitioners justify not valuing time to cultivate themselves? Indeed, nothing pleases the buddhas and bodhisattvas more than doing your Dharma practice—listening to and contemplating the Dharma and meditating diligently to cut off attachment to this life.

In traditional Chinese opera, male and female characters and jesters represent divergent personas in the ordinary world. Practitioners must reflect on the kinds of roles they are playing. Those who assume only perfunctory, virtuous roles but do not cultivate internal qualities are no different from the jesters, the laughingstocks of the world. But it could be worse. A jester in a play will at least inspire laughter in the audience. The jesters among practitioners, however, benefit no one and ruin themselves and others.

How should we perform our parts? Do we play to the audience with fancy dances and movements, or are we genuine and solid in practice and realization? Shouldn't we ponder these issues deeply?

May 19

Joyful Always

SUFFERING can be naturally transformed when one's practice reaches a certain level. The secret to remaining joyful when encountering any obstacle or misfortune is to relax the mind. Tsangpa Gyare says: "A mind steeped in attachment can never be free from avarice, hatred, and pain. If you learn to stop clinging and relax the mind, happiness will never depart from you."

A great yogi in Tibet, Chekhawa Yeshe Dorje, mastered sutras and tantras and possessed genuine bodhichitta. In a life of seventy-five-year years (1101–75), he founded Chekha Monastery and took nine hundred disciples under his care. He instructed his followers: "Always maintain a joyful spirit and guard your mind at every moment. To hold oneself as truly existing is the cause of all troubles; instead, think always to repay the kindness of all sentient beings. These are the supreme pith instructions to practice." That is, we should remain peaceful every minute and look into the nature of the mind in all our activities, whether sitting, standing, sleeping, or moving about. When difficulty arises, do not blame fate or others. Dispel self-cherishing and exercise the Four Immeasurable Qualities. Even when we have nightmares, we should apply the view of emptiness rather than try to eliminate them. Thus, we remain unattached in all circumstances.

Geshe Khapa said: "If you don't know what activity to adopt and what to abandon, nothing you do will bring happiness; if you're wise enough to know, adverse conditions facing you will become supporting ones." Therefore, the way to happiness is to maintain the correct view while being attentive to our conduct.

Geshe Langri Tangpa says:

> Live a simple and humble life in a solitary place; give up amass-
> ing possessions meaninglessly.
> Devote yourself to virtue day and night; give up the futile
> search for relationships.
> Stay put in your room and tame your own mind; give up fol-
> lowing people aimlessly.
> Please your teacher by practicing the Dharma as an offering;
> give up chasing hollow fame and fortune.
> Protect others by offering assistance; give up reciting useless
> wrathful mantras.

A restless mind is exhausting, while contentment brings peace. When a person's mind is imbued with a positive attitude, a brilliant surge of light will shine forth from within. Wherever one goes in life, showers of happiness and a sense of ease will always follow behind.

May 20

Essential Points

THE THREE SUPREME METHODS—the very pith instruction to enhance the accumulation of merit—is stressed by all the great masters, whether during a large, general teaching or a one-to-one transmission. Patrul Rinpoche has repeatedly admonished his disciples: "Whenever you do something positive, no matter how big or small, it is essential to enhance it with the Three Supreme Methods. In the beginning, generate bodhichitta as a skillful means to make sure that the action becomes a source of good for the future. In the middle, do the main practice free of concept or reference, which prevents the destruction of merit by circumstance. At the end, seal the action properly by dedicating the merit, which ensures that it continually grows ever greater."

Omniscient Dharma King Longchenpa in *The Precious Treasury of Pith Instructions* also left this teaching: "Beginning with the motivation of bodhichitta, you go beyond the Basic Vehicle. Practicing without attachment, you realize the nature of emptiness. Concluding by dedicating the merit, free from the three concepts, you transform all activities into the path." And in *The Great Chariot: A Treatise on Finding Comfort and Ease in the Nature of Mind,* he says: "Always perform any meritorious act by arousing bodhicitta in the beginning, abiding in non-conceptual wisdom while doing it, and at the end dedicating the dreamlike merit. Understand that any positive action done with the Three Supreme Methods is called 'the virtue that leads to liberation' and is the cause of complete enlightenment. On the other hand, any positive action done without the Three Supreme Methods is called 'the virtue that leads to temporary happiness.' Its merit will be exhausted after bearing fruit only once."

Therefore, if our goal is to attain perfect buddhahood, all our positive actions—reciting mantras, making offerings, reading books, liberating captive lives, doing prostrations, and any other seemingly insignificant ones—should always be accompanied by the Three Supreme Methods. Like a drop of water falling into the ocean, merit dedicated to enlightenment will never dry up until its goal is reached. In the *Middle Prajnaparamita Sutra*, the Buddha says: "Shariputra, dedicate the merit solely toward total enlightenment and do not dedicate it to anything less, such as attaining the level of a shravaka, pratyeka-buddha, or others."

Although I always preach these instructions, I myself have failed many times to execute them. How embarrassing! Lama chen!

May 21

The Key

TO OPEN the gate of any treasure chamber, we need the right key. Even more so, to access the splendid treasure of the Buddha's teachings requires the golden key of wisdom. Simply saying "Open Sesame!" ardently will never grant you entrance to the treasure chamber.

With his infinite love and compassion, the Sublime Conqueror endows whatever he says with various levels of meanings—outer, inner, secret, direct, or indirect—so that sentient beings of different capacities will understand and fulfill their aspirations accordingly. Only the Buddha possesses such unique abilities of verbal expression. No one else has them, be they an erudite scholar, the best-informed expert, a world-famous intellect, or even an arhat who has eradicated all negative emotions. Therefore, the seeming contradictions in Buddhism—such as understanding one as many, many as one, certainty as uncertainty, or appearance as emptiness—are all the Buddha's teachings to suit infinite beings at the apparent or hidden level. With detailed analysis, a wise person can see that these teachings do not conflict with one another; instead, they are full of profound meaning. *Praises to Buddha's Speech* says: "Yea or nay, one or many, certain at one time, uncertain at the other time—none of these are at odds with one another." Hence, only with wisdom can we comprehend the adamantine words of the Buddha and establish the ultimate versus the provisional meaning, the four intentions, and the four secrets.

Where is this key to opening the speech treasure of the Buddha?

The omniscient Longchenpa hid it in the lines of the eighth chapter of *The Great Chariot: A Treatise on Finding Comfort and Ease in the Nature of Mind*. But alas, people these days are just too busy to spare time looking for the key!

May 23

A Lipstick

A MAGAZINE ARTICLE says a woman worker spent 300 yuan from her 500 yuan monthly income just to buy a brand-name lipstick. Reading it, I can't help sighing deeply. Leaving aside the issue of how she can manage her other expenses for the month, to pay such an exorbitant price for this kind of item makes no sense.

I have never cared for heavy makeup. We have these sayings: "Out of water arises the elegant lotus flower, and its natural beauty needs no embellishment." And, "With no powder or ointment applied, such is the fresh face of Chang'e." Spending 300 yuan on lipstick is not as good as using it to save captured fish or birds, make offerings, or buy books. Remember, a perfectly sculpted and adorned face will not last forever. No matter how you make yourself the fairest of all—an elaborate hairstyle, delicately arched eyebrows, lustrous red lips, and gleaming white teeth—all will erode as time passes. There is no avoiding the fact that a rosy face will wrinkle and ebony hair will fade to a white mess. Ouyang Xiu laments in the *Ode to the Autumn Sound*: "Thus, his ruddy complexion is withered and his black hair turns white." In the end, a pile of gristle and bone.

A wise person should avoid turning oneself into someone "having a rotten interior beneath a fine exterior." The grandest ornament comes from cultivating one's virtuous qualities and wisdom. Devoting oneself to study, reflection, and meditation on Dharma is better than wasting time and money on outward beautification. Who wouldn't feel reverence toward monks or nuns whose every act shows grace and propriety? Who would think of a loving and kind older adult with creased skin and thinning gray hair as an eyesore?

The only unfailing ornament emerges from realizing the nature of the mind. It is so sad that people still can't distinguish the real from the fake. I want to tell them: Give up pointless decoration. Seek only true beauty!

May 24

Dream Glimpse

PEOPLE who live on a lonely mountainside yearn for a busy city with its continuous stream of crowds, cars, and activities. While city dwellers, myself included for the moment, miss the quiet and peaceful life in the mountains.

Turning off the desk lamp and closing my eyes, I fell fast asleep. As it's said, what you dream at night is what you have thought during the day: In my dream, I was living in a quiet mountain cave that was simple and tidy inside. Outside the cave were big trees and stunning flowers; eagles soared in the sky, carried along by the gentle breezes; squirrels scurried around as if playing with the running brooks; yellow roses brimmed over with bright sunlight; and in the morning mist, crystalline dewdrops fell from the tips of tree leaves. Here I led a carefree life like an innocent child, and time passed quickly and quietly. Then one day, a little monkey showed up in front of me. I promptly took out my best food to treat him, my only guest. After the meal, the monkey somehow was unwilling to leave. Perhaps he had been separated from his mother, or a hunter had captured his mother. Anyway, I had no choice but to adopt this poor little fellow.

With my patient training, the little monkey learned to prostrate, make water offerings, burn incense, etc. When I read books, recited a sutra, or chanted mantras, he would play quietly nearby, not causing trouble. When he acted disobediently on occasion and I shooed at him, he would immediately behave and do prostrations. We ate the rice cooked in the same pot and lay on the same big flat rock during breaks. Wherever I went, we were always together. The monkey brought much joy to my practice life, never disturbing my peaceful mind.

One day I had to walk down to the base of the mountain for food. Though it wasn't necessary, I ordered the monkey to stay and watch the little hermitage. The monkey looked at me gloomily and settled reluctantly on the stone slab by the door. When I glanced back some distance away, his tiny lonely figure was still there. Suddenly I woke up and everything was gone; nowhere was the cave or the little monkey. Worrying about the poor little thing and missing the tranquil life in the cave, I tried hard to journey back to my dream, but to no avail.

The Great Biography of Shakyamuni Buddha, the White Lotus tells a story: A person kept an elephant while practicing in a secluded place. The god Indra was displeased and reprimanded him sternly. Therefore, it seems inappropriate for spiritual practitioners to keep pets. But somehow, I still miss the monkey in my dream intensely. Perhaps he is still waiting earnestly for my return!

May 27

Sad Reflections

MANY GREAT BEINGS, either accomplished spiritual masters or extraordinary worldly intellects, often endured hardships and gained no recognition during their lifetime. It's as if their qualities were non-existent before their death.

Once when Rigdzin Jigme Lingpa was in deep meditation at the mountain hermitage, he had a vision of Longchenpa. He asked: "Oh, Omniscient Great Master! I have prayed to you so ardently all these years, but why haven't you appeared to me before now?" Longchenpa answered: "It is only now that you all address me as the Omniscient One! When I was alive, I could hardly sustain my basic need for food and clothing, let alone be called the omniscient!"

Indeed, that's how things go. An authentic teacher usually keeps a low profile, conducting himself modestly and attracting no attention. Even if he accepts disciples, they do not fully realize their master's qualities. Only after the teacher's death do the disciples recall his greatness. But by then, it's too late. Nowhere can they find their teacher again, and they are overcome with acute remorse and longing.

Our kindest Guru Jigme Phuntsok Rinpoche once said: "Only after I die will your faith in me increase. Things like this have happened to many others; I am no exception." It is the same in worldly affairs. As it is said: "There are plenty of fine steeds around, but astute talent scouts are hard to come by." Gifted individuals often have to suffer poverty and extreme hardship before being recognized.

Beethoven, the dynamic composer who merged classical and romantic music styles, experienced many adversities—serious illness, utter poverty, etc. He became so outraged when he once lost a mere penny that he poured his emotions into the piano piece "Rage Over a Lost Penny." How destitute and hapless he must have been! Schumann, deeply moved upon hearing this, wrote an elegant article to commemorate it.

Cao Xueqin, who penned the legendary masterpiece *Dream of the Red Chamber* (The Story of the Stone), endured the extreme poverty of living only on weak broth.

Emperor Liu Bei of the Shu Kingdom made three visits to the thatched cottage of Zhuge Liang to request his assistance. His eagerness to seek talent, like a thirsty person searching for water, is rarely seen in the world, now or in the past. Many unsung heroes could only lament that their genius remained unrecognized and their dreams never fulfilled.

What would be the use of glorious posthumous recognition to dead persons if they were not acknowledged during their lifetimes? To spiritual seekers, it is more significant to appreciate the teacher's excellence while the teacher is still alive.

May 28

Two Truths

"FORM IS EMPTINESS, emptiness is form; form is not other than emptiness, emptiness is not other than form." This verse is often quoted by people who know little or nothing about the Dharma, usually with much relish and an air of smugness. When asked what emptiness or form means, they are entirely ignorant, or at best, they think "form" is related to color or a woman's figure, while emptiness is a complete void.

It is of paramount importance to comprehend the true meaning: form and emptiness are not different. The correct view of the two truths is indispensable at any level on the Dharma path, be it the Shravaka, Pratyekabuddha, Mind Only, Middle Way, or Vajrayana school.

The *Fundamental Wisdom of the Middle Way* says: "The right view is absolute; the worldly view is illusory." The nature of fundamental absolute space is the union of awareness and emptiness. From the non-existence of anything, myriad phenomena arise. Due to ignorance and obscurations, sentient beings engender wrong views and cycle in samsara endlessly. If one realizes the indivisibility of luminosity and emptiness and achieves the acceptance of non-arising phenomena, pure inner radiance will manifest in its entirety.

The notion of absolute and relative truths is the cardinal point in Tibetan Buddhism, and as such, it is the main topic for thorough analysis in debate and logical reasoning. The luminary masters in the Nyingmapa tradition have left numerous peerless teachings on realizing the two truths.

Longchenpa, the Dharma king, says in *The Great Chariot: A Treatise on Finding Comfort and Ease in the Nature of Mind*: "The two truths do not exist separately like the two horns of the bull. When the moon is reflected in water, the moon's appearance is relative; that the image has no inherent existence is absolute. Appearances and emptiness are non-dual, the union of the two truths."

Besides the Middle Way, the highest Great Perfection further elaborates on the two truths—primordial purity and spontaneous presence. *The Treasury of the Supreme Vehicle* says: "On the relative level of appearance, it is called *thogal*, based on spontaneous presence; on the absolute level of emptiness, it is called *trecho*, the "primordial purity." The so-called two truths are not separate entities but are of the same nature, relating to different aspects, like a person who is a Brahmin and a precept holder at the same time." Rongzom Pandita also said: "One who has realized the non-duality of the two truths, seeing no difference in things and the natural state of things, is called a practitioner of the Great Perfection, a master in view and action." These pith instructions from the lineage masters of the Great Perfection, Longchenpa, and Rongzom Pandita, are most precious to those with deep faith and wisdom.

Wisdom is the direct cause of accomplishment, while virtuous activities provide supporting conditions. On the Dharma path, we develop prajna wisdom in absolute truth and diligently accumulate merit in relative truth through numerous positive activities. Wisdom and merit enhance each other; neither is dispensable, and this is the way to perfect enlightenment.

May 29

Bidding Goodbye

THE GORGEOUS flowers that brazenly showed off all spring and summer are now withering, their fallen petals scattered like snowflakes, reduced to mud under the wheels or crushed to dust when stepped on. So ephemeral are all the beauties in this world—blink, and they are gone. Just as the wilting of spring blossoms or the falling of autumn foliage shows the impermanence of the universe, so the fading of a pretty face or the blanching of black hair reveals the impermanence of human life.

If we do not accept the lesson of impermanence revealed by nature, we will squander our precious human life, which is as brief as a dewdrop or a flash of lightning. Bound by the rope of delusion, we hoard wealth, possessions, friends, and relatives while not preparing for death. When suddenly confronted with the final moment, we will likely make fools of ourselves in all sorts of ludicrous ways. Consider Yan Jiansheng in *The Scholars*, who died with the everlasting regret of having lit one too many oil lamps.

The Buddha has imparted 84,000 ways of making the best use of our life and dying prepared. As all roads lead to Rome, we need only pick one and practice it consistently and diligently.

Life and death, samsara and nirvana, are by themselves equal. There's no arising or cessation of the Buddha, and no difference between the mind's nature and the Buddha. Realizing this, one abides in the natural state that is the Buddha and attains the ultimate liberation by eradicating delusion and crossing the torrents of cyclic existence.

This meditation state may be too lofty for ordinary people. For them, Mipham Rinpoche left his profound instruction: "For those who have not yet attained a high level of meditation, simply by thinking of Buddha Shakyamuni once, they will be reborn in the Pure Land of Great Bliss." Therefore, at the time of death, praying to Buddha Shakyamuni or Buddha Amitabha with unwavering faith can ensure your rebirth in the Pure Land. However, clinging firmly to possessions or loved ones will make you fall short of success during the last stage, despite years of mantra recitation.

May 30

Human Ocean

HERE IS an immense ocean populated by people of diverse colors speaking different languages. Huge tides of this human ocean rise and fall unceasingly, generating continuous, roaring waves that pound the shore. Those good at surfing ride high and have fun; the less skillful are carried adrift by tides or are wiped out, settling to the bottom. These are our worldly affairs, with their never-ending ebb and flow; driven by karma, people are forever busy, running hither and thither. I cannot help but let out a deep sigh, thinking how miserable we humans are!

A master of the Six Yogas of Naropa taught the following: "The eight worldly concerns occupy our human minds; the pursuit of happiness, especially, has become the common denominator among all living beings. There is no one in the world who does not chase after their desired objects, busily running around and toiling day and night. Yet in truth, behind all sources of happiness lurks inevitable suffering. Hence, there's no need to feel joyful when happiness comes or dismayed when suffering befalls us. We invest huge amounts of energy or resort to unscrupulous means to satisfy our cravings in this life, only to ruin our future lives for sure. Coveting bountiful pleasure and enjoyment, we will do anything—Dharma or non-Dharma—for this life only because we are shortsighted people, trapped in the eight worldly concerns! Everyone should reflect deeply on this! Future generations should also heed this warning. Be cautious; do not make the same old mistakes!"

Like ripples on the water, everything we chase after so tirelessly and wholeheartedly will vanish in no time. If we don't wholly renounce the avaricious mind, trivial affairs of this life will happen endlessly—just as the next ripple comes up as soon as the previous one disappears. Wouldn't it be wise to cut down on our activities and chattering? Sakya Pandita says: "Unless you let go of all your worries and concerns, all sorts of events will arise and keep you constantly busy and distracted. Becoming engrossed in one triviality after the other, when will you realize that you are throwing your life to the wind?"

It is clear that no matter how we struggle in the frightful turbulence of the human ocean, we will never come out intact without being bruised or injured. A wise man, therefore, should choose to free himself from the bondage of worldly concerns. The *Treasure of the Void* states: "Give up home and possessions; cut off chasing after money and meaningless pursuits. Set out to secluded hermitages deep in the mountain and live your life like a wild animal." Wish not to become a spectacular wave in the vast human ocean; to escape from it quickly is the only wise choice.

May 31

June First

TODAY IS Children's Day in China. Kids are out playing and celebrating. Seeing their innocent, beaming faces reminds me of my experience on this special day. Until I went to elementary school at age fifteen, I had not received any formal education and had never heard about Children's Day. I remember it was an unusually bright and sunny day. While not technically a child any longer, I managed to mingle with a group of authentic children. We sang songs together and waited for nearby herders to give us yogurt, which we had long been craving. Being much older, I was almost as tall as the teacher, yet I had to pretend to act like a child. It's still amusing to recall what I went through that day. Later, I moved on to Zong Ta Middle School, which signified the end of my childhood period.

Today, I'm already in my forties. My childhood, free from worries, sorrow, or burdens, has become a remote memory, like a dream. However, I feel fortunate to have become a Buddhist over the years and to have met many sublime teachers who will continue to drench me in the nectar of Dharma throughout my remaining years.

How are my childhood friends doing these days? Sometimes I wonder. Are they as lucky as I have been? How many of the children I saw today will be able to enjoy the sweetness of Dharma? The answer may be only partially satisfactory. Due to a lack of proper guidance, many children will likely end up in the same rut as their parents—afflicted by karma, delusion, and negative emotions, thus wasting their precious human existence.

How fondly I remember one Children's Day that I enjoyed in a Buddhist region where children were nourished by the Dharma, both at home and in school! On this particular day, they acted out the Buddha's life stories and teachings on a small school stage. Though naive and simple, their performances nonetheless planted virtuous seeds in their minds and would prevent them from veering onto an unwholesome path in life. If this tradition of celebrating Children's Day can be promulgated worldwide, how wonderful it would be!

June 1

Flickering Candlelight

A CANDLE FLAME flickering in the wind is likely to die out at any moment. This simile applies to the fickle faith of some practitioners toward the Three Jewels when encountering adverse situations. Lacking a solid foundation, they are likely to lose faith and even beget wrong views and commit non-virtues. Therefore, it is most critical to start one's Dharma practice by relying on authentic teachers and, through listening and reflection, establishing a faith unassailable by the eight winds of worldly concerns. On this basis, if one engages in practices to eradicate mental fabrication with wisdom and abides in the state of thusness, one arrives at a rare and most admirable stage.

Khenpo Depa is my kind teacher who initiated me onto the Dharma path. The preliminary practice I received from him has been the bright light guiding me in the big ocean of Dharma. The Great Perfection he transmitted to me is a priceless jewel coming down through an unbroken lineage from Longchenpa, Mipham Rinpoche, and many great masters of the past. The mere sight of his slight and frail figure always aroused in me ever-deepening faith. Starting in his youth, he relied on many teachers and has worked strenuously in his study, reflection, and meditation on the Dharma. Not only has he mastered the *Five Major Treatises* and the profound tantras, but he is also well-versed in the science of using music in communications and in fine arts and crafts.

From age twenty-eight to forty, he was deported to do herding and woodworking and was incarcerated during that politically chaotic period. Despite all these trials, his Dharma training never stopped.

While herding, he would hide the leaves of text around his waist and study hard whenever he chanced upon a secluded moment. On woodworking duty, he labored painfully during the day, and at night, doors and windows shut tightly, read until midnight under a dim light.

I was twelve when I first met him. Dressed in a gray outfit, he told me that in the current situation, a Buddhist should never forgo reliance on the Three Jewels. To guard our mindfulness and the flame of faith amid the furious storm, pray wholeheartedly to our teacher and the Three Jewels. As he said this, a ray of golden sunshine streamed through the window, shining on his rosy and wrinkle-free cheeks. I was struck by a warm feeling welling up from the bottom of my heart. As I look back, scenes of that day still leap before my eyes as vividly as ever.

In 1983 the political turmoil abated. The learned and compassionate Khenpo Depa began teaching at his woodworking shop in the town of Upper Lekhogma, and that's when I completed the five preliminaries of the Great Perfection. Finally, before him and Lama Ruga, I donned the monk's robe and began my journey of no return toward liberation.

As a practitioner, will I be able to emulate Khenpo Depa—to uphold and protect the torch of Dharma from dying out under all adverse circumstances?

June 3

Omniscient King

THE OMNISCIENT SOVEREIGN of Dharma, Longchenpa, is a manifestation of the primordial Buddha Samantabhadra. Every single word of his teachings is pure gold. Having the connection to read or hear his teachings is a result of merit accumulated throughout countless eons, and it is a fortune to be rejoiced in immensely.

Jamyang Lodro Gyatso says: "In India and Tibet, there have been many great scholars and highly realized beings. But none of their works and commentaries could ever surpass those of the Omniscient Longchen Rabjam." Longchenpa says: "The teachings I expounded on are exceptional and hard to come by, and among them you can easily find instructions for profound realization."

Patrul Rinpoche also advises ardently: "The more you read other commentaries written from conceptual thinking, the more concepts you will spawn. On the other hand, merely listening to one sentence of the self-arising commentaries that go beyond any mental fabrications will effortlessly bring you meditative concentration. To study the concept-bound commentaries is entirely in vain. Longchenpa's teachings are like the wish-fulfilling jewel that grants people lasting joy and peace. They are imbued with the same blessings as those from the Buddha. The merit of hearing, reflecting, or meditating on them is just as great. How marvelous! How amazing! I pay sincere gratitude to the masters of the three transmission lineages. By seeing, we establish connections; by practicing, we create vast merit. Buddha nature is within every sentient being. How true that is."

Many people nowadays immerse themselves all day in books written from discursive thoughts that only exacerbate the ills of the three poisons. Why not spend more time browsing the treasure trove of Longchenpa that manifests his supreme, absolute wisdom?

June 4
Written while reading "A Treasure Trove of Scriptural Transmission"

On Competition

HUMANS LOVE to compete. We never tire of competing to see who is better, whether in international affairs, economics, politics, sports—the World Cup, the Olympics, and so on—or personal achievement and honor. It doesn't matter if the competition concerns radical transformation or the most trivial matter; people habitually plunge into it. Although there is no live ammunition and artillery in these contests, the smell of gunpowder permeates them. They are wars masquerading as competitions.

Driven by karma, many people are propelled into competitive activities, exhausting themselves all day long. Moreover, they often set unrealistic goals that are tough to reach, inevitably falling into a pit of inextricable agony. When seeing people around them get promoted, become rich, go abroad, or even buy an outfit, they feel an indefinable sense of loss. To satiate their thirst for feeling superior, they will try every possible way to get the better of their opponents, causing the economic crime rate to rise and increasing social unrest. In all, they are doing more harm than good.

A person who returned from his Lhasa pilgrimage recently told me about a practitioner named Lei Gong who has recited the Vajra Guru mantra a hundred million times. Lei Gong told his fellow pilgrims that his cave was in Yamalong, near Samye. Surrounded by mountains and limpid streams, it is warm in the winter and cool in the summer. A sparkling mountain spring gave him sweet drink, and ordinary tsampa tasted like ambrosia. His life is calm and unfettered, free from attachment and worries.

In comparison, worldly people always run around and compromise their integrity for scanty material gains. Their hard work all day long brings nothing but negative emotions. How miserable they are indeed!

Practitioners in name only also like to watch or participate in competitions. They willingly bear the anxiety from these contests but cannot appreciate the happiness of practicing in solitude. They constantly rush about tending to superficial virtuous activities, and their minds are restless from being tempted by power and money.

As a Dharma practitioner, can I be just like Lei Gong—renouncing worldly fame and wealth and abiding only in the bliss derived from Dharma? Will I always be able to stay calm and unwavering in this ever-changing world?

June 5

Yogurt Treat

WITH THE APPROACH of summer comes yogurt, the best delicacy in the Tibetan pastureland. There is a saying in my hometown: "A summer without yogurt is akin to a field devoid of vibrant colors." Indeed, should "no yak, no yogurt" happen to any household, it would be lamentable.

Like anyone growing up near a pasture, I have a special affection for yogurt. Since I am now staying in a Han Chinese area far from my hometown, I thought I would miss the yogurt treat this summer. Thus I was pleasantly surprised today when a lay friend brought me local yogurt. It was almost as delicious as that from the high pastureland. Moreover, some of the yogurt had fruits mixed in, giving it a unique flavor. As I enjoyed the yogurt, my mind flew back to when I had it with my beloved guru on June 28, 2000. At that time, H. H. Jigme Phuntsok Rinpoche was in retreat at South Mountain (Nan Shan) and teaching Tibetan lamas on the Great Perfection. I led a group of monks, nuns, and lay people from the United States, Singapore, and Mainland China to pay a formal visit to him. Our car made tracks through the rugged mountain passages. Upon reaching the top of Nan Shan, we saw our guru's little cottage surrounded by a dazzling array of colorful flowers. With the vast blue sky as a backdrop, it was a perfect scene from any angle, and everyone could not help exclaiming: "Oh my, it's so beautiful!"

In this picturesque setting, we all paid homage to our teacher, who appeared to be in good spirits that day. He had each of us served yogurt, which was placed into our hands, and he took some into his hands too. He said: "Yogurt was the best food that sustained me during my schooling when I was young; I am offering it to you today. Although we have no serving bowls here, we can still enjoy this delicious yogurt from the bowls of our hands. A little austerity poses no problem to us practitioners." And then he took the lead and ate the yogurt from his hands with relish. As I began eating mine, happiness from the heart gushed out like a fountain.

I still remember every moment of that day as if it had been yesterday. I yearn for the day I will be with our guru again, sitting on the pastureland, enjoying the tasty yogurt.

June 6

Aspects of Dharma

THESE DAYS, only a few individuals understand the Dharma well and put it into practice. Still, others proclaim themselves to be Dharma practitioners despite lacking systematic study and basic Buddhist knowledge. Isn't it a joke?

Master Vasubandhu, widely revered as the second Buddha, says in the *Abhidharmakosha Shastra*: "There are two aspects in Buddhism: the Dharma of transmission and the Dharma of realization. The Dharma of transmission relies on language, while the Dharma of realization requires practice." In other words, the Dharma of transmission is made possible by teaching and listening, while the Dharma of realization is attained through actual practice. These two Dharmas, transmission and realization, cover all dimensions of the Buddhadharma.

For the Dharma to remain, we must rely on sutras and shastras. The *Sutra Requested by Deva Ruyi* says: "The Dharma entails sutras and shastras that are the wonderful teachings of the Buddha and the commentaries on the implicit meanings, respectively. Through them, the Dharma will last long in the world." The teachings of the precious Tripitakas reveal our innate buddha nature and help us to recognize it. Due to ignorance, all sentient beings have had their true nature obscured. Unable to realize that phenomena perceived by the six senses do not exist ultimately, they commit negative actions through delusion and suffer as a consequence.

With no Dharma guidance, it's like setting off on the road with no sun, moon, or any light source by which to navigate our course; we end up cycling endlessly in the suffering of samsara. Or, like a blind person with no escort, we can only wander in the barren desert of the three worlds with no hope of escape, however hard we may try.

Once we comprehend the root cause of samsara, we should study and practice the Dharma authentically. Integrating the three higher trainings—discipline, meditation, and wisdom—into our being, we eradicate our obscurations and confusion and grow our merit and wisdom to a remarkable extent.

Although buddha nature is innate to us, it is obscured, like the gold in the ore, the flame in the unlighted match, or the seedling in the rice grain. Without smelting, striking, or planting, no realization is ever possible. If we don't practice what we know intellectually, we are like someone who describes delicious food without eating it or counts others' money without possessing it himself. There is no real benefit at all. Having drifted in the ocean of samsara for countless eons, if we lightly gave up this once-in-a-lifetime boat of liberation, we would never be free.

Neither the Dharma of transmission nor the Dharma of realization is dispensable. Through the Dharma of transmission, we establish the right view; on this basis, we engage in practices to attain the Dharma of realization. This approach is the authentic way to train in Buddhadharma.

June 7

Wooden Bowl

K HENPO NGORPA offered me a gift of a wooden bowl purchased at a specialty shop at Xiamen Botanical Garden. The bowl, coated in a clear varnish over its natural wood grain, looks simple and unsophisticated. I like it and use it to eat my everyday meal, and to me, any food, once placed inside the bowl, turns into something nectar-like. As my affection for this bowl grows, I recall a story about Patrul Rinpoche.

When Jamyang Khyentse Rinpoche was in Derge, Patrul Rinpoche was wandering from place to place in the guise of a beggar. He carried a wooden bowl with him over the mountains and valleys of the Kham area as well as to many remote places. Having kept company with Patrul Rinpoche through the ups and downs of his life as a vagabond, the bowl became his favorite.

When he formally visited Khyentse Rinpoche, he saw that the master kept a large entourage and lavishly ornamented his palace-like house with gold, silver, and jewels. Patrul Rinpoche thought: "It seems that the master enjoys material goods and he must be quite attached to this houseful of treasures." Khyentse Rinpoche clairvoyantly saw what had gone through Patrul Rinpoche's mind. He scolded him and got right to the point: "Patrul! Don't imagine things! My clinging to all the treasures in and out of the house is far less than your clinging toward your wooden bowl!" This sentence pierced Patrul Rinpoche's heart, and it dawned on him that living austerely does not make one special. What counts is to give up any grasping internally.

As ordinary practitioners, it's even more pressing for us to renounce cravings for wealth and glory in the world. Instead of planting virtuous seeds or connecting to the Dharma, many covet money and power, thus enduring tremendous anxiety and worries. Too bad it's rarely acknowledged that we are only temporary caretakers of our possessions, at most for decades. Why cling to them? Saraha says: "Any clinging, even as tiny as desiring a sesame seed, is the cause of cyclic existence."

Therefore, feeling disgusted, we should ditch all attachments as we would when trying to break free from jail or shackles. Otherwise, no matter how diligent we are, it will be in vain, exhausting our body and mind.

June 8

Got It?

KHENPO DEPA'S writings covering every stage of the spiritual journey have been compiled into four volumes. Today I would like to offer Dharma friends my translation of his advice in the form of thirteen questions, which begins:

I am sharing my thoughts with those who, through collective past karma, now perceive similar and confused appearances. Whoever has faith may access this teaching.

1. To cross the vast ocean of samsara in our short life span, the only thing we can rely on is this precious human body. But when we age, our faces will be entirely wrinkled. Do you know that?

2. The world—cities and monasteries—and the beings within it— high officials and retinues, gurus and disciples—are all teachings on impermanence, and they don't stay long. Do you know that?

3. A person who kept pure precepts and taught the Dharma earlier could later become a secular person with kids. Without the armor of genuine renunciation, one betrays his hidden self. Do you know that?

4. One can impressively preach the Mahayana doctrine while the demon of self-interest plagues the mind. The loud proclamation of empty bodhichitta is like the frantic yelping of an old dog. Do you know that?

5. Without cultivating a pure unbiased view, you regard someone you don't know as a guru or receive tantric instructions indiscriminately from anyone. These are the causes of hell rebirths. Do you know that?

6. Complaining about the turbidity of our times, you still go along

with it and engage in hideous conduct. The inviolable law of karma overrides even the most stringent worldly laws. Do you know that?

7. Saying that everything is empty, you belittle causality. Although samsara and nirvana are empty, appearances will infallibly manifest through interdependence and are capable of performing their respective functions. Do you know that?

8. Having no realization of the inseparability of great purity and equality, you heedlessly transgress precepts in the name of tantra. You throw yourself into the dark abyss. Do you know that?

9. Without attaining any accomplishment, you freely appropriate the goods of the sangha or offerings for the dead. In Yama's Hall, you must repay this with your flesh and blood. Do you know that?

10. After the poor person dies, charlatans devoid of quality busy themselves with death rituals, ruining themselves and others. Performing authentic transference for the dead requires wisdom and skillful means. Do you know that?

11. People proclaim that they have taken refuge in Buddhism and consider themselves superior. However, it is impossible to germinate the fruit of merit on an arrogant iron ball. Do you know that?

12. We are spiritual siblings under the care of authentic and kind teachers. We must take the pain and pleasure we feel in samsara with an equanimity that corresponds to our level of realization. Do you know that?

13. The above questions are not meant to be judgments that pick on others' faults. Instead, they are mirrors to check on our good and evil. Do you know that?

June 10

Revered Master

I T HAS BEEN over a month since our beloved Guru Jigme Phuntsok Rinpoche was hospitalized at 363 Chengdu Hospital. Today, Dodrupchen Rinpoche, coming from Sikkim, is visiting our guru.

Before his arrival, our guru specifically told us to prepare a nice seat for our guest. Presently Dodrupchen Rinpoche, an elder in his eighties, walking unsteadily, came in with an attendant. He declined to sit on the seat prepared for him but instead sat on a small stool, prayed for the long life of our guru, and described the development of Buddhism in India and China. They then started chatting about various things, religious and not, shifting from one topic to another. So animatedly were they engaged in talking that they showed no signs of fatigue.

Our guru asked Rinpoche how many attendants he had when he traveled abroad. Rinpoche replied: "None. I went all by myself." "That's it? But who took care of you on the way?" "I have people meeting me on arrival and sending me off on departure. It's a hassle to have someone accompanying me. Please don't be fooled by my age; I am still well enough to care for myself." Incredibly, this highly renowned master of Tibet prefers to keep a low profile, which contrasts glaringly with so-called masters who lack realization but surround themselves with massive entourages.

Thus, these two great spiritual masters enjoyed their heart-to-heart talk and together made aspirations to remain in the world to benefit sentient beings. Rinpoche also blessed us before heading to his lodging at Shudu Mansion Hotel. When we got there, many followers from various regions were waiting respectfully for him.

At the moment we parted, Rinpoche purposefully entered a short meditation and urged me to do the following practices to pray for our guru's long life and to remove hindrances for the guru and disciples: 10,000 recitations of the *Prayer to the Eighteen Arhats*, 100,000,000 recitations of the *Heart Mantra of the Four-Faced Buddha Mother*, and 100,000 recitations of the *Tantra of Stainless Purification*.

I take to heart what he said and hope we all work seriously and earnestly for the long life of our guru and all accomplished masters. May all obstacles and unfavorable conditions be dispelled!

June 12

Real Patience

I WITNESSED an impressive scene today at a five-star hotel. A patron got into a fuming rage and almost punched a female employee. However, the attendant retained her graceful, professional smile throughout the rampage, and her composure was admirable.

Patience, or forbearance, is the most difficult of the Six Transcendent Perfections to keep. Exercising patience when dealing with sentient beings is never-ending training for every Buddhist. The scripture says: "Patience is the foundation of keeping pure precepts and attaining quiescence. The growth of all good qualities relies on patience." However, many Buddhists, myself included, cannot compare with this female hotel employee. If an ordinary person can practice exceptional patience for the sake of a paycheck and career, how can a Mahayana practitioner, who aspires to work for the temporary and ultimate happiness of self and others, lag behind? Shouldn't I feel quite ashamed?

Theoretically, we all know that good and bad actions we have accumulated cause us to experience happiness or suffering. When confronted with an outraged person, we should not blame anything else but our past evil deeds. Longchenpa says: "If a karmic debt is due, one cannot escape retribution, and if no karmic debt is due, there is no repayment. In addition, praise or slander from others carries little weight in benefiting or harming us."

When we are punched or scolded by someone, instead of seeing that person as an enemy, which most people would do, we should regard the person as a spiritual friend. By understanding the causality principle clearly, we will not be provoked to a knee-jerk response, hastily labeling others as friends or foes. It is commendable that this attendant displayed such a remarkable degree of forbearance. As a result, she will surely enjoy its marvelous fruit in the future.

The scripture says: "Patience cuts off evil at its root; it also pacifies all those who are quick to reproach." If we can practice bodhichitta and patience when being wronged, our karmic debts and evils will be exhausted and uprooted, and we will attain ultimate happiness.

June 13

Blessed Objects

LIKE MANY people, I care very much about objects that have been blessed. I always wear my most cherished ones and rarely show them to others except my closest friends.

Some people feel that this kind of attachment is unwarranted. Given that all phenomena are like a dream, an illusion, a bubble, or a shadow, why make such a fuss about the blessed objects? Indeed, from the point of view of absolute truth, everything is pure and equal. However, the power of these things is unfathomable from the viewpoint of dependent arising.

I remember visiting Dilgo Khyentse Rinpoche in Bhutan in the nineties on a sweltering and humid day. Although Rinpoche was bare-chested, he wore a gau box and other amulets around his neck. He opened the gau and told us that the image of Manjushri was the very Manjushri that often emitted light and melted in Mipham Rinpoche's heart when he was composing shastras. Rinpoche then blessed us with the gau box, filling us with tremendous joy and gratitude.

Likewise, our beloved Guru Jigme Phuntsok Rinpoche has always kept his treasure-filled gau with him, taking it off only when bathing. In the Kagyu lineage, the black hat of the Karmapa is a priceless treasure respected by thousands of people. The Zen sect of Buddhism, renowned for its doctrine of "no clinging whatsoever," still has its sacred Dharma gown that is passed down from one lineage holder to the next. The fact that great masters placed extreme value on sacred objects reveals the mysterious power of interdependence beyond our ordinary minds' comprehension.

After his nirvana, Buddha Shakyamuni left us many rare body relics to worship and pay homage to. Scriptures also state that wearing sacred ornaments, images, or texts on our bodies will protect us from evil beings and hostile forces. Therefore, until we realize the unity of purity and equality, it is prudent not to disparage the significance of sacred objects.

June 14

Offering Blood

AS I STOOD by the window watching many people outside rushing here and there, my mind started wandering. All of a sudden, a buzzing sound cut short my thoughts. A brown-white mosquito alighted on my arm. So, it's you, the noisy one! Soon it drew its snout and pierced my arm. I began reciting Avalokiteshvara's heart mantra, wishing for the mosquito's swift liberation. At the same time, I entertained myself with its cute way of feeding. The mosquito, maybe afraid of losing its rare feast, appeared completely absorbed and cast no side glances. Soon its slender abdomen rounded up. Only then did it decide to withdraw its mouthpiece, ever so satiated. Perhaps because of being too full and heavy, it wiggled up and down my arm a few times before taking off with a wobble. The humming resumed, but unlike earlier, it vibrated with a happy overtone. Strangely, even a mosquito in a good mood can make a pleasing sound.

Immediately, I recited the dedication prayer Buddha Shakyamuni uttered when he offered his flesh and blood to evil spirits in his previous life:

> By this merit may all beings attain omniscience.
> May it defeat the enemies of wrongdoing.
> From the stormy waves of birth, old age, sickness, and death,
> may we free all beings from the ocean of samsara.

Indeed, my offering of a minute amount of blood to a mosquito is in no way comparable with the great deeds of the Buddha. But as the saying goes: "Although water droplets are tiny, they will gradually fill a huge container." An ordinary person can accomplish only small virtuous deeds, but by accumulating them bit by bit, the day of reaching the same state as the Buddha will undoubtedly arrive.

June 16

Taste of Luxury

A LAYPERSON told me that he always stays at the most deluxe hotels when he travels. He insisted on treating me to a stay at a five-star hotel so that I could get a taste of its lavish amenities. Thus, I was booked into the top hotel in Chengdu, the Jin Jiang.

From the moment the cab pulled up, the meticulously individualized services of a five-star hotel switched on. The bellhop opened the door for me and picked up my luggage. Stepping into the lobby, my eyes were enticed by the glittering décor. In my room, the elegant furniture, comfortable large bed, and spotless bathroom promised a pleasant getaway.

The restaurant displayed full spreads of sumptuous Chinese delicacies and other exotic cuisines to whet the appetite. I enjoyed the feast in an atmosphere of soft melodious music and imagined that by popular standards, such an experience must be one of the topmost pleasures in life. However, I couldn't help but wonder how the expenses of my stay would compare to the cost of saving the lives of tens of thousands of eels. Wouldn't it be wonderful if this money were used to release live beings instead?

Lying on the luxurious bed, I recalled this tale from *Stories Old and New*: A certain wealthy man feasts on the nicest dishes of every kind throughout the day, but at night he suffers from nightmares of being thrown into hell, enduring tremendous torture. On the other hand, even though he eats rotten food and sleeps on hay, his shepherd boy always has blissful dreams in which he enjoys celestial happiness. The rich man offers to trade dreams with the young herder. Even though the rich man has to do hard labor and eats only spoiled food, he doesn't mind because blissful dreams await him at night. At first the shepherd boy indulges in lavish pleasures during the day, but soon he grows weary of the nightly tortures. When they become unbearable, he returns to his shepherd's life. Therefore, a luxurious bed doesn't guarantee a good dream, while a makeshift bed in the open meadow may offer a delightful nightscape.

Drifting in my thoughts, I fell asleep. When I woke up I discovered that although I did not have bad dreams, the fancy soft bed hurt my poor back for a long time.

June 17, at midnight
Written while fighting back pains on the carpet in the Jian Jiang Hotel

Young Nephew

I HAVE MADE a point of not mentioning my relatives in this diary. But the news I heard today was just too much for me to contain and I am giving in and writing it down here.

My nephew Rigdzin Norwo is ten years old and, as I recall, is quite frugal. I have been giving him a little pocket money each month, and he always holds on to it tightly. When his peers buy snacks or soft drinks, he is a bystander. Even if he is drooling and quietly swallowing his saliva, he still resists spending any of his money on snacks. He is a real scrooge and tries to beg or borrow his daily necessities from all possible sources.

Yet today my brother told me that my nephew offered all the money he had so painstakingly saved over a long period, 600 yuan in total, to Khenpo Tsultrim Lodro for animal liberations and blessings. He kept not a single penny for himself. I was deeply touched. Rigdzin Norwo has a propensity for kindness and loves to set captured animals free. Once, he was severely injured by a tractor. To console him, I said, "You know, had it not been for your constant practice of releasing live beings, you could have sustained more fractures." He agreed and said, "I thought so too. I am very grateful for the blessings of the Three Jewels."

Although my nephew has deprived himself of the pleasure of savoring snacks, his gains are immeasurable. Many of his young peers, already conditioned to worldly ways, do not hesitate to harm others out of self-interest. When they encounter bad luck, they become distressed and blame fate or other people. My nephew's otherwise sensible conduct must be credited to the blessings of lamas and the Three Jewels.

I wish my nephew's peers would have the same fortune as his so that the light and rain of Buddha's teachings would always nourish them. May they be spared from the violent storms of mundane existence, and may they not repeat the same mistakes of their predecessors. As to my nephew, I can't foretell his future, but at least for now, his actions have brought me immense joy.

June 18

Leaving Chengdu

IT HAS BEEN eight months since our beloved H. H. Jigme Phuntsok Rinpoche left Larung for medical treatment in Chengdu City. Although the *Uttaratantra Shastra* and other scriptures say that sublime beings are free from aging and illness, great masters still display signs of physical decay. They do so to demonstrate impermanence and provide opportunities for sentient beings to cultivate merit, thus freeing them from the demonic grip of ignorance.

A few days ago, our Lama Rinpoche mused: "Thousands of my students in Larung have been earnestly waiting for my return. I must fulfill their wishes, no matter what. Let's go back!" Thus, at seven this morning, a dozen of us quietly left Chengdu and headed toward the home we've long been missing, Larung Valley.

Rinpoche, still in poor health, started to throw up shortly after we departed. The situation worsened when entering Wenchuan County, so we had to pull off the road. On a rug spread over a field, our master's vomiting continued. Even though our hearts ached with painful anxiety, we were powerless to ease his ordeal.

Across the field, sheer cliffs rose toward the sky like a fateful barricade blocking our way home. The nearby river powerfully surged on, as turbulent as my agonized soul. Woeful tears welled up in my heart, and they flowed into a sad melody:

> The green mountain shoots high up into the clouds,
> the raging river keeps raising turbulent waves.

As our dear teacher suffers from an unrelenting illness,
how we disciples feel unbearable agony and pain!

Had the four groups of disciples at Larung known of our guru's current condition, many would not have hesitated to sacrifice their own lives in exchange for his health. But here, bearing witness to our guru's haggard appearance, I was at a loss as to what to do. For now, we had to forgo our earlier plan to stay in Li County and go to Wenchuan instead.

June 19, at Wenchuan

Limiting Sleep

THESE PAST few months, on health grounds, I have forsaken my habit of rising early, and I sometimes still linger in bed even when it is already late in the morning. The fact that Dilgo Rinpoche maintained his habit of sleeping very little for decades and never gave in to any excuses makes me feel deeply ashamed.

Having vowed to serve all beings, I must value time, limit my sleep, and diligently advance on the path that brings true benefit to myself and others. The scripture says: "Great sages sleep less and constantly engage in ways to awaken; they give up indolence, entertainment, earthly desires, and physical adornments . . . While others are indulging in pleasures, the wise remain diligent. Staying awake while others are slumbering, the wise, like fine steeds, overtake the lesser horses." In other words, we should cut down on sleep, eliminate meaningless pursuits, and practice vigilantly toward the unsurpassed state of awakening. While most people are in oblivious slumber, the wise are wide awake. Like a fine steed galloping way ahead of slower horses, a practitioner who never slacks off and always stays fresh will be the first to reach the finish line.

It is commonly said: "Everything is imitation; he who does best is he who imitates best." As an ordinary person, although I cannot emulate the admirable conduct of the sages, at least I can follow their example of sleeping less.

June 20
Miyaluo

Sweet Reunion

WHEN Yeshe Phuntsok and Tsultrim Lodro learned about the imminent return of our guru to Larung, they wasted no time rushing to Shang Zhai to await him. Yeshe Phuntsok arranged for a lodge for our guru, supposedly the best in the area. However, this so-called top accommodation did not live up to its name.

Tsultrim Lodro, Zhe, and I squeezed into a room that needed cleaning. The floor was scattered with cigarette butts and garbage, and the pillows and sheets were filthy. Yet the pleasure of reuniting with long-separated old friends made this stay no less enjoyable than the recent one at the five-star hotel. The dinner also turned out to be quite delicious; indeed, the power of the mind transcends everything.

While taking a stroll together after dinner, we passed by a new residence built on a lot where the locals used to slaughter yaks. Tsultrim Lodro said with a sigh: "Isn't the human being an awful creature! Had this place been an execution ground for people, no one would have imagined building a house here and calling it home, yet they don't care about the animals' plight at all." Feeling that the unhappy souls of many slaughtered yaks must be lingering around, we recited mantras for them and dedicated the merit for their rebirth in higher realms. On a hilltop facing the building, many prayer flags printed with Avalokiteshvara's mantra were flapping in the wind, echoing our prayers.

After sprinkling its final golden glow on the hills, the sun disappeared on the horizon and night fell in Shang Zhai. Back at the lodge, there was no water or basin. A loud snoring, clearly audible through the thin walls, beat on my eardrums like a melodious lullaby; it quickly sent me to the realm of sweet dreams.

June 22

Welcoming Home

V ERY EARLY in the morning, I woke up excited that we would return home soon. Opening the window, I took in the fresh air bursting with vitality. The season of extended daylight and dancing butterflies has arrived. The sky was pristinely blue with no trace of clouds, and all the trees were budding green. The rising sun drove away hazy mists, sending golden dust on the ground. Basking in this morning's glory, we left Serba and began our return to Larung in an impressive procession.

Villages and monasteries along the way had all heard the good news of H. H. Jigme Phuntsok Rinpoche's return. The crowd lined up at the sides of the road, holding katags as they waited respectfully. All eyes were moist with tears when the car window came down and our guru waved to them. The year-long acute yearning for Rinpoche finally dissolved into misty puffs, spiraling gently up into the blue sky.

Arriving at Huoxi, thirty motorcades joined the head of the procession, followed by a cavalry of a hundred adorned stallions ridden by strong, athletic young men. With the master's car in front, the imposing parade of more than a hundred ornamented cars stretched as far as the eye could see. This stream of joy brought overflowing waves of happiness wherever it arrived.

The parade reached its highest point when the cars arrived at Nuo Ruo village. Monks from Larung Academy dressed in yellow robes formed two lines along the road, like two long celestial ribbons. The hill slopes were full of people, and the green mountains seemed dyed the golden color of the monks' robes. Day and night, everyone had been waiting eagerly, gazing at the road continually to catch sight of their master on his way back. It was the moment of realizing their dream, but they did not know how to express the joy erupting inside them. The thousands of words that welled up in their hearts became excited calls or soundless weeping.

Our guru delivered no speeches due to tiredness, but his return was more than enough. Everyone felt the warmth and security of the guru's presence, just like babies returned to the cozy embrace of their mothers.

The setting sun ushered in the Milky Way; the night veil of millions of stars closed over the field. Although the night was still bitterly cold on the prairie, everyone in the tents dreamed the same sweet dream, as their hearts had all been warmed.

June 24

On Deathbed

THE WEATHER was getting muggy and black clouds hung oppressively in the west. It seemed like it was going to rain. By the roadside, quite a few corpses were waiting for sky-burial at the Larung burial site, darkening my mood like the gloomy sky. But as the saying goes, "Nothing is everlasting. How can this sack of flesh and bones be an exception?" We are all mortal. Sooner or later, I will be in the company of these corpses, rushing toward the netherworld. Will I know what to do when that moment arrives?

I am fortunate to be endowed with this human existence and to have met the Dharma and our incomparable guru. Nonetheless, my involvement in worldly activities has often prevented me from seriously engaging in practice. Having experienced life's changes and witnessed enough human dramas of sorrow and joy, I fully appreciate these sayings: "Secular vanities are like bland foods. Days and years pass swiftly like a shooting bullet." It is high time for me to make preparations for my final departure.

From beginningless time, we have committed innumerable misdeeds due to ignorance and stupidity. It will prove quite impossible to gain liberation from the rounds of birth and death if we rely on our own power alone. As taught, if one doesn't know what to do when dying, the best bet is to remember one's guru. Spiritual teachers embody the Three Jewels; to think of them is to think of all the buddhas throughout space and time. The *Sutra Requested by Miao Bi* says: "As death approaches, remembering the guru for even a mere second is the best way to die. One will be assured to attain liberation." Thus, no matter how severe our sins may be, recalling our root guru at the moment of death will bring rebirth to a pure land and buddhahood.

A grain of sand will sink when placed on top of the water. When loaded on a giant cargo vessel, boulders weighing thousands of tons do not sink but can reach the other shore. Likewise, by calling Buddha Shakyamuni, Buddha Amitabha, or our root gurus on our deathbeds, we will board the best ship and sail directly to the Pure Land of Ultimate Bliss. Will I be mindful enough to remember all of them when dying? Lama Chen!

June 26

Traveling About

"TO WEAR OUT cushions by sitting on them is better than to wear out shoes by traveling about." I always employ this adage to encourage myself. Many practitioners take pride in becoming roaming spiritual seekers and happily busy themselves with pilgrimages or visits to Dharma centers. One day they pull up to a temple for a short overnight stay; the next day they are on a pilgrimage to a sacred mountain. But I have my reasons to disapprove of such itineraries. Patrul Rinpoche reminded us: "Sightseeing at sacred mountains or going on pilgrimages for pleasure seems to be a spiritual practice, but it's not."

Before realizing thusness, the main focus should be on taming one's mind rather than drifting around like a rootless weed. If we allow circumstances to scatter our minds all over the place, we will surely waste this most precious life. Suddenly, aging and illness butt in uninvited, but it will be too late to cry over spilled milk.

Even if one wants to travel, doing so mentally without laboring the body is more advantageous. Hidden in book pages are all three thousand worlds. The *Avatamsaka Sutra*, for instance, is a complete tour guide of the cosmos. While staying put, one's imagination can journey at will through the infinite Avatamsaka cosmos. It is far better than taking trips that tire our body and mind. Armchair traveling in books saves one from encountering bad weather, landslides, earthquakes, bandits, wild beasts, and even the danger of losing one's life or possessions. I urge you to check it out.

Genuine spiritual seekers, will you think over my suggestions?

June 27

Vital Essence

All phenomena arise from causes,
these causes have been taught by the Tathagata,
as well as that which puts a stop to these causes—
this too has been proclaimed by the Great Shramana.
Abandon evildoing.
Practice virtue well.
Master your mind.
This is the Buddha's teaching.

THIS VERSE encompasses all the essential points in Sutrayana
Buddhism. Practitioners can benefit all concerned by explaining
its meaning to others and reciting it when receiving offerings or dedicating the merit of animal liberation.

"Abandon evildoing" comprises the core of Shravakayana: one must
maintain one's integrity and not harm others. "Practice virtue well"
embodies the essence of the Bodhisattva path—that is, to embrace all
beings in the world and engage in beneficial activities:

- relieving beings from suffering
- helping those in need
- caring for the lonely
- being patient with others' faults

"Master your mind" refers to purifying the mind's obscurations and
eliminating all negative thoughts.

If practitioners follow this instruction, benevolent gods will always protect them and no evil spirits can harm them. Many joyful and auspicious conditions will spontaneously come together. Their aspirations—to pacify afflictive emotions, to escape the rounds of rebirth, and to attain enlightenment—become quickly within reach.

The poet Bai Juiyi once implored the Bird Nest Zen Master:

"Master, what is the essence of Buddhism?"

"Abandon evildoing, practice virtue well," the master answered.

"That's it? But even a three-year-old knows this."

"A three-year-old might know it, but an eighty-year-old can't really do it."

That is how things usually go; it is easier said than done. We need to redouble our efforts to put this teaching into daily practice.

The Buddha and his disciples often recited this verse to dedicate the benefactor's merit when receiving offerings. Tibetan monks used to do the same, and some Thai monks still say this verse when receiving alms, which I learned during my trip to Thailand in 1999. This practice is now falling out of fashion for some reason. Many monks will say thanks but nothing more after partaking in meal offerings. As this tradition came down from the Buddha's era, we better not let it die out. Let us restore this good practice to bring out its many benefits!

June 29

Life's Junctures

OH DEAR, stop being lazy. Shape up and do your translation! Making myself a cup of jasmine tea, I picked up a pen and turned the pages of the scripture. However, instead of translating, my mind began to play out the scenes of my life one by one.

The time as a shepherd boy: White clouds sailing in the blue sky over stretches of green fields, I ran barefoot with other boys, singing happily. We had hundreds of yaks as our close friends, and we enjoyed ourselves to our heart's content, roaming over the vast undulating terrain.

The time as a schoolboy: I was like Ali Baba, who stumbled upon the secret cave where forty bandits had been hiding their treasures. Carrying my book pack, I walked into school with my classmates and heartily collected many jewels from the chamber of knowledge.

The time as a monk: Donning a monk's robe and in the company of thousands of spiritual friends, I came under the care of our guru. We studied and contemplated sutras and shastras; we surfed in the vast ocean of sacred Dharma, purifying the obscurations of our body and mind.

The time as a translator: As fate would have it, opportune connections happened with many Han devotees. Keenly wishing to share with them the precious treasures of Tibetan Buddhist teachings, I became determined to translate its essence into Chinese. With pen in hand, I buried myself in the scriptures, spending numerous days and nights delving deeply into my thoughts and racking my brain.

Now it should be my time to enter the practice phase. When Master Atisha arrived in Tibet, he asked Rinchen Riwo's help in translating. The veteran translator replied: "Can't you see my hair is turning gray? I should not spend time on translation anymore, and I must do my practice." The master admiringly agreed: "Indeed, it's time for you to practice." These days, my hair is much grayer than before. Lacking authentic meditation, what I know remains on a superficial level without melding into my mind. If I do nothing about it, I'll soon arrive at the death phase and become history.

June 30

Graceful Exit

TODAY a monk from Qinghai told me the news that Lama Topden passed away a month ago. Lama Topden was a disciple of Dzogchen Khenpo Kunze and had made a secluded retreat in the mountains for twenty-one years. Even in prison he held to his practice. His profound realization often caused auspicious signs of accomplishment to appear. He wrote *The Great Perfection: Cloudless Spacious Sky* (which I am privileged to have read) and trained scores of outstanding disciples.

He was rather ill toward the end. On the day he died, he told people around him: "All you students connected to me, here is my advice if you will listen: You must practice bodhichitta diligently when I am gone." Thus, he ceremoniously put on his formal gowns, sat in the vajra posture, and serenely passed away.

In Vajrayana circles, numerous tantric practitioners can foresee the time of their own death and make a graceful exit. Moreover, receiving empowerments and Great Perfection pith instructions will confer long-term benefit. Even though disciples have yet to achieve realization in this life, they need only to uphold unfailing faith and strictly observe the tantric vows. In future lifetimes they will meet Vajrayana again and reach attainment due to the blessing of having heard this sublime Dharma.

Now that we have encountered this supreme teaching, we shall arouse faith and devotion a hundredfold, generate the unsurpassable bodhichitta, and practice assiduously to deliver all bewildered sentient beings.

July 1

Human Flying

TAKING WING, birds fly in the vast sky. The legend that "the fabulous roc soars for thousands of miles" depicts the carefree gliding of that mythological bird. It also reflects the idealistic gentry's yearning for a pristine state. Since antiquity, humans have been dreaming of making headway against the pull of gravity and rising into the immense skies. Lin Daiyu, weary of the bitter and biting ways of the world, cries out in the *Dream of the Red Chamber*: "May a pair of wings grow under my arms. May I fly with flower petals to the limits of the sky." A prayer in an ancient rite says: "Opening the gate of heaven, I ride on heavy black clouds; whirls of wind lead my way, and rainstorms clean the road ahead of me."

Numerous folk tales speak loudly about the human longing to fly. There are figures of flying deities in Dunhuang frescoes. Ancient legends also depict Chang'e flying to the moon and the seven fairies descending to the human world. Most people regard these stories as nothing more than fantasies and think that it is impossible for humans to fly without the support of an airplane, a balloon, and so on.

However, human flying is not just a fairytale. Vajrayana has many authentic historical accounts of flying in a human body. According to *The Nyingma School of Tibetan Buddhism: Its Fundamentals and History*, by Dudjom Rinpoche, there was once a nun called Manmo who, after a tsog offering, rose together with her two disciples to the sky and flew toward the Pure Land of Guru Rinpoche. Nearby shepherds witnessed the unusual sight and, after partaking in the tsog offerings, all attained unsurpassable samadhi. As recently as the 1950s, in broad public view, Khenchen Tsewang Rigdzin levitated and flew to the Pure Land a day before his political persecution was to take place.

Near the end of the Harvest Festival at Larung, Khenpo Tsultrim Lodro left and traveled around the clock to find witnesses to authenticate this tale. After tramping across mountain ridges for hundreds of miles, at Yushu, Qinghai, he met the old leaders of the persecution at the time of Khenchen Tsewang Rigdzin. In the interviews, they repeated to him what they had seen with their own eyes: the sight of Khenpo rising from the yak he was seated on. All those at the scene witnessed this extraordinary spectacle.

Today Khenpo Tsultrim Lodro told me about these interviews that he will compile in detail. The article should be out soon. Whoever reads it—those skeptical of human flying or those studying Vajrayana—will no doubt develop faith in the achievements afforded by Vajrayana. Don't miss this article!

July 2

Spurring On

A KHENPO who has just returned from India told me about his four years of study at Drepung Loseling Monastery. Drepung has about three thousand monks. Every morning at five they are roused from sleep by the wake-up bell, and the day consists of a heavily packed schedule until eleven at night, with very few breaks in between. In this high-intensity learning environment, unforgiving whips will surely reprimand anyone who dozes off or goes against the rules.

All students are subject to a rigorous and progressive education program. The first-year curriculum includes basic Buddhist logic (Hetuvidya), which entails studying the knowledge gained through the senses and by inference. Next is seven years of study on the *Ornament of Clear Realization*, three years on Madhyamaka, and four years on the *Abhidharmakosha*. The *Compendium of Valid Cognition* runs through the entire program. Everyone must learn sixty prose chapters or more by heart; failing that means expulsion. Only after a student finishes all these curricula in the Sutrayana and passes strict examinations and evaluations can he embark on the secret Mantrayana studies.

As the saying goes, a man of unmistakable worth naturally attracts admiration. The monastery's strict and nearly oppressive administration has attracted elites worldwide and has graduated many preeminent monks.

The khenpo's description of his experience stirs in me a great respect for the administrative system of the monastery. I have grown lazier over the years because there is no external pressure on me, and my sloth and distractions have killed my numerous plans to read books or undertake tasks. As a person lacking self-discipline, I could use a fierce outer whip to incite my diligence, rattle me up, and force me to progress.

July 3

Nearing Death

A STRANGE DISEASE has struck my childhood friend Yuno. Half his face started to swell up inexplicably. The ailment compresses the nerves, affecting his daily living and threatening his life. All treatments have proven ineffective, and his situation is beyond medical intervention. Having no choice, he left his children and hometown and came to Larung to await the final verdict from the Lord of Death.

I visited him today and was shocked to see his distorted face, which revealed no trace of his handsome and youthful self. Hearing my words of consolation and good wishes, he forced a smile, which made his face even more gruesome. It's almost impossible for me to associate the Yuno in front of me with the Yuno in my memory as a happy shepherd boy.

We were merry and carefree back then, herding yaks together in the pastures. Early in the morning, we set out with the rising sun and misty fog; late in the day, we returned home under the rosy clouds while singing folk songs. Yuno had been the handsomest and liveliest among the bunch of us. Yet time and tide have washed away the enchanting days, and now coming face to face with my childhood buddy, it all seems so long ago.

Life is full of fickle joys and sorrows. Misery often comes after fun; bleak wind and rain always sneak up behind sunny days. Unless one finds Dharma as a saving grace, one will be helplessly blown about by unrelenting karmic winds, landing in the treacherous intermediate state and waiting in confusion for an unknown future.

Yet it is a consolation that out of this calamity Yuno chooses to make Buddhism his refuge. Simply by his faith and devotion, he'll die prepared. It has been said: "Extreme happiness in the god realm prevents celestial beings from attaining enlightenment; miserable suffering in the human realm facilitates humans to attain buddhahood." Heavenly beings indulge in extravagant pleasures and exhaust their merit, resulting in their ultimate downfall and cutting off of buddhahood. Conversely, suffering in the human world, though painful to endure, acts as a warning and a spur, leading humans onto the path of liberation.

With skillful methods, we can transform diseases into prescriptions for liberation and unfavorable conditions into favorable ones. I wish Yuno all the best and pray that he will understand these teachings.

July 4

Quiet Contemplation

A SHOWER enlivened the grass as if with a spray of green dye. Flowers on the front porch and in the backyard bloomed lavishly. Sitting in the yard, I turned the pages of the *Ratnakaranda Sutra* and read this passage: "To attain a peaceful and supple mind, a beginner should train in a solitary place." Indeed, until one has realized the unity of appearances and the mind, one should avoid distracting surroundings.

Longchenpa also states: "Before gaining stability in meditation, a person's mind is easily disturbed. Therefore, one should remain in a tranquil place." By initially practicing in solitude, one melds the teacher's pith instructions into the mind and sees that all activities of walking, sitting, standing, or lying down are none other than practices, and nothing goes beyond the display of Dharma. When one perceives that the universe, mountains, oceans, and galaxies in all directions are transparent and pure appearances, one will be able to accomplish any task effortlessly.

The great Geshe Shardong of Jakhyung Monastery says in *Essays on the Stages of the Path to Enlightenment*: "If one has become immune to external ills and has melded the Dharma with the mind, then spreading the Dharma in big cities such as Beijing or Tianjin is a feat worth rejoicing in. However, those lagging in such realization had better continue meditation alone."

Listening attentively in the yard, now and then I heard only birds flapping their wings while gliding through the sky. Silence reigned everywhere. Looking around, I sensed a calm and subdued surrounding but for the flowers showing off unabashedly in the yard.

Larung Buddhist Academy is the home of thousands of Dharma aspirants. Through the incredible blessings of our beloved guru and the Three Jewels, people here are committed to taming their minds. Realized practitioners still hide their accomplishments and keep a low profile, making Larung Gar an alcove that attracts many spiritual seekers. I feel utterly fortunate that I am on this serene land and can be a member of this community!

July 5

Venerating Guru

TODAY I had the privilege of reading a concise biography by the great wisdom being Shapkar Tsogdrug Rangdrol of his spiritual master, His Holiness Chogyal Ngakgi Wangpo. Every vajra song composed by Shabkar is in praise of his master, revealing his incomparable devotion to his guru.

His Holiness Chogyal Ngakgi Wangpo was a Mongolian monarch whom Shabkar met for the first time at a vajra festival. The master sat on the lawn with his consort, enjoying the carnival shows. Shabkar paid homage to the master and was accepted as a disciple. He then embarked on practice, first studying the stages of the path to enlightenment and then receiving empowerment in the secret Mantrayana and transmissions for the supreme *Seven Treasures*. When he was preparing to go on solitary retreat, his master said: "Our days together are numbered, do not go away." He listened and followed his guru to a secluded place in which to practice together. During that period he circumambulated the guru's tent daily, and the guru's blessing strengthened his faith.

Later the guru permitted him to practice meditation at Qinghai Huxin. He sealed his retreat cave with boulders and mud, locking himself up and practicing relentlessly. One night he dreamed of a man riding a blue steed who told him: "Your master is going to another land. Don't you want to see him?" Without a second thought, he joined the man to go to his guru's place.

By the time they reached their destination, his guru was nowhere to be found. He asked the man on the blue horse: "Where is my guru?" "He is now in the Dakini Land of Freedom," the horseman answered as he whipped the horse and galloped on with tremendous speed. After a long ride, Shabkar saw tens of thousands of people holding precious parasols, jeweled umbrellas, gongs, and drums in a procession welcoming his master. Bowing to the master of his endless yearning, with tear-filled eyes he implored: "Master, please take me with you!" His guru said: "Not now. You have to go back and meditate. You should strive to benefit beings." The master then blessed him and went on his way. Presently, inconceivable numbers of gods and goddesses streamed out from the sky, respectfully greeting his guru. He kept his eyes on his master until the huge entourage disappeared. When he woke up, his pillow was wet with tears. He learned later that his master had passed away on the very same day.

How marvelous are the blessings of realizing the wisdom-mind lineage! May I arouse the same strong faith as that of Shabkar in his guru!

July 7

A Dream

IN MY DREAM, I came to the Jiaga area of my old herding days. For seven wonderful days and nights, I was in the presence of an emanation of Avalokiteshvara from India, whom I served with reverence, always staying right next to him. He wore his regular outfit, and his every gesture was imbued with kindness and warmth, fully revealing the quality of an authentic spiritual friend. I couldn't help but feel drenched in wordless bliss at every moment.

Seven days went by in the blink of an eye. On the last day, he told me he would like to leave me a few teachings. I was beyond ecstasy. I had been secretly hoping for good luck but was too timid to ask, knowing my lack of merit and the defilements of eight worldly concerns. Now that my wish would be granted, how could I not be overjoyed? I humbly handed the master a blue pen and saw him writing on the pad: "Build your view on Madhyamaka, direct your activities to benefit others . . ." He summed up the essential points of all the doctrines in two and a half pages. He scribbled at first and then wrote more neatly. After finishing, he handed the pages to me and let me pay homage to them. When he placed the scriptures on my head, I sought his blessings. He recited the aspiration prayer in *The Precious Treasury of Pith Instructions*: "In all my lives, wherever I am born, may I obtain the seven noble qualities of the higher realms. On being born, may I meet the Dharma and have the freedom to practice it in the right way . . ." His voice was initially resonant and clear and then grew faint and indistinct. Even as I write, the dream remains vivid, as fresh as if I were still in it. I remember bowing down, my downcast eyes meeting the soft glow from his reddish-brown shoes, which was beautiful to behold.

Fortuitously, the next day when Khenpo Shebul helped me straighten up my place, he found a gift given to me by the master that had long been missing.

I have told this story intending to share my happiness, and I speak only the truth without the slightest intention of bragging. Please take it for what it is worth.

July 8

Giving Dharma

GIVING DHARMA means helping others on the spiritual path by explaining the Dharma, transmitting the texts, etc. If done with pure intention, it is highly meritorious. The *Sutra Requested by Kimnara Tongpor* says: "The Buddha told Ananda: 'By giving the Dharma, one pacifies afflictive emotions; by offering material goods, one begets a strong physique. Giving the Dharma confers one with thirty-two qualities, such as developing wisdom and gaining the power to conquer lust, hatred, and ignorance.'"

Explaining the Dharma widely to others is an act of immense generosity. Even clarifying a single verse for merely one or two persons is commendable. The *Sutra Requested by Maitreya* says: "The Buddha said to Maitreya, 'Suppose someone had filled as many world systems as there are grains of sand in the Ganges River with seven precious jewels and offered them as a gift to the Tathagatas of the ten directions, and suppose someone else with a compassionate heart had elucidated but one Dharma stanza to others. Then the heap of merit accrued by the former does not approach a billionth part of that of the latter.'" The benefit of teaching the Dharma is obvious.

Even advising someone to read or browse through the scriptures is also a way of giving the Dharma, and lay practitioners can accomplish this and earn immeasurable merit. In the *Perfection of Wisdom in 8,000 Lines*, the Buddha says: "Suppose a son or daughter of a spiritual heritage had caused others to read a Dharma discourse, bear it in mind, or practice it—the strength of that act would amass a great heap of merit, immeasurable and incalculable."

Worldly tradition deems personally serving and caring for one's parents the foremost filial piety. To the heir of Buddha Shakyamuni, attaining enlightenment and benefiting beings is the supreme act of piety to repay kindnesses. Therefore, we should strive to spread the Dharma so that all beings in the six realms are freed from suffering once and for all. In this way, we can repay the kindness of our innumerable parents in our past existence for giving us life and raising us. And at the same time, we also propagate the wisdom lineage of the Buddha's legacy, a responsibility none of us should shirk.

July 11

Karmic Connection

A LAY PRACTITIONER from Xiamen visited me today. Upon seeing me, he earnestly implored me: "Dear Lama! You must grant me your blessings, as my liberation depends on you, my venerable master!"

I often hear this kind of pleading. Irrespective of my meager ability as an ordinary being, even if an accomplished master or the Buddha appears in person, they cannot throw you and me into the Pure Land like catapulting stones up into the sky. Were that the case, the Buddha, with his immense compassion, would have liberated all of us with no one left behind in the Saha world, and samsaric sufferings would have long disappeared. But why are we still here?

Without effort on our part, there is absolutely no hope for liberation. The *Sutra of the Discipline* (the *Vinaya Sutra*) says: "I have already shown you the way to liberation, but your liberation depends on you, so exert effort." We ourselves hold the key to our future. Due to our heavy negative karma, we have not been saved by the inconceivably great numbers of buddhas that have already come. Now that we have met our precious gurus and received the supreme method of liberation, we must follow the instructions with unrelenting resolve.

A water container turned upside down will not reflect any moon image. Likewise, a practice devoid of effort and devotion will not resonate with the Dharma or trigger the blessings of the Three Jewels. As it says in the *Avatamsaka Sutra*:

The moon is shining high up in the sky,
yet no reflection appears in unsuitable vessels.
Likewise, the moonbeam of Buddha's great compassion
will not reach those lacking karmic connections.

Without the convergence of requisite conditions, even the Buddha can appear to be powerless; yet we can create the most propitious conditions by practicing assiduously.

July 12

Helpful Teaching

AFTER LUNCH, I closed the gate and made offerings of incense and butter lamps at the shrine. When everything was in order, I began my favorite activity—reading. The sky was neither cloudy nor sunny, mirroring my mood of the day. The chirping of birds outside the window, the buzzing of bees among flowers, and the ticking of the alarm clock on the table all accentuated my surrounding's quietness. Turning a page of the *Sutra of Fearless Offering Samadhi*, a passage caught my eye:

> I should regard every being as the Supreme Teacher. Why? Because I do not know who among them has successfully tamed the mind or who has not done so.

Indeed, as ordinary beings, we cannot tell a realized great siddha from an everyday person. As buddhas and bodhisattvas often manifest in various forms to help sentient beings, we better regard all beings as buddhas and treat them with respect before we attain the wisdom of discernment.

The *Jewel Heap Sutra* also states:

> Kashyapa, only I and others of the same caliber can see through phenomena and sentient beings. Ordinary people cannot do so, and acting on false assumptions will cause their downfall."

Moreover, all sentient beings have buddha nature but appear differently due to various degrees of confusion. Nonetheless, by dispelling the clouds of confusion, the wisdom moon will eventually emerge in full view. Hence, I must pay obeisance to all future buddhas.

This short passage benefits me tremendously. Will I be able to conduct myself according to it from now on? At the very least, I have made my aspiration to do so today.

A knock on the door broke the silence of moments ago. It's time for me to go out and take care of things.

July 13

My Birthday

ON THIS DAY forty years ago, I arrived in this world with a cry in a yurt overlooking a prairie. Now, four decades have sped by like a gusty wind or a lightning bolt, and my days as a baby awaiting feeding, an innocent boy, or a vigorous youth have all disappeared like a dream. What remains indelibly in my mind is my parents' kindness in giving me life and raising me. Moreover, I am in debt to my precious guru, who, with loving tutelage, has cemented in me an unshakable heartfelt faith in the Three Jewels.

I rejoice that, to celebrate my birthday, many Dharma friends all over the country are releasing captured live beings on a considerable scale. Thousands of yuan are being donated in Mongolia, Beijing, and other places to save various animals and creatures. Numerous lives are thus snatched to safety from the jaws of death; it is a worthy effort, even though some may deem it otherwise.

To satiate their appetites and palates, deluded humans with mighty power recklessly kill weaker species and plunge them into the abyss of misery. However, all living creatures—those in the air, on land, or in the water—without exception have feelings and senses, just like you and I. Their desire to live differs not from yours or mine, even though they cannot speak out. Humans who rashly kill other innocent beings behave like beasts—is there any difference? Now that we have this precious human existence through our past virtues, even if we cannot abstain from meat, we must at least perform the good deed of lifesaving.

In the future, should anyone arouse faith after reading my writings or translations and wish to express gratitude, there is no better way to please my departed soul than to release doomed, captured animals.

July 14

An Old Woman

ON MY WAY to get a shot at the Hospital for Aiding the Poor, I saw an older woman wearing rags in front of a store. She looked pleadingly at passersby while tightly holding two-yuan bills in her hand. Her face, beaten by the bitter elements and covered with heavy layers of dust, was pale and ashen; her eyes, stricken by an empty stomach, hungrily searched here and there.

The day was sunny and pleasant. Passersby, preoccupied with their shopping lists or errands, were oblivious to the existence of this older woman and trampled mindlessly over her already filthy skirt. No one cast a single glance in her direction.

When I was done at the hospital an hour later, I walked by the same spot and saw that the same drama continued. I took out the only ten-yuan bill I had and placed it in her hand. Her eyes began to fill with tears, but I could not bear to look into them and hurriedly fled, leaving behind me an old figure murmuring something with palms pressed together.

Seeing the insensitive crowds passing around her, I wished I could have said a few words to them: "Be nice to this old lady! Don't you know that we will also become old and ailing in misery? Why not try to put ourselves in her shoes now?"

After returning home, my back pain worsened. I thought about the old lady: What is happening to her now? How will she manage to eat tomorrow? Alas!

July 15

Staying Healthy

"DO TAKE GOOD care of your health!" These days, people always greet me with this bidding, as if my health has become the weightiest issue on Earth. I often remind myself of the axiom "sound body paves the road to great achievements" and keep up my daily health care, lest poor health should hinder spiritual training.

A report I read today gives the World Health Organization's definition of health: "Health is a state of complete physical, mental, and social well-being and not merely the absence of disease or infirmity." Reading this, I immediately felt relieved. So, as it turns out, I can be counted as relatively healthy compared with many others. At the very least, I have not been troubled by a lack of coordination, mental imbalance, maladjustment, or restlessness. The body influences the mind, but mental factors also considerably affect the body. For myself, ailments in my body's components—bones, flesh, blood, or internal organs—have often plagued me. Still, these minor physical miseries are nothing compared with the mental agonies many others suffer.

Typically, we tend to attach excessive value to our physical body. Striving for its comfort, we painstakingly fight in the worldly arena and scheme for gains down to the last detail, our minds becoming restless and our emotions confused. Excessive clinging to the body drives a person to pursue wealth and fame instead of studying, contemplating, and meditating on the Dharma, which is a massive obstacle on the path. But our flesh and bones do not really belong to us, and all

phenomena in the world are illusory. Only by letting go of our attachment to the body and protecting our minds from corrosive emotions
can we become truly healthy.

July 16

An Auntie

ONE OF MY aunts who had been very kind to me when I was little is ill. Upon hearing the news, I hastened to pay her a visit. She is living in an unthinkably shabby place; other than a dirty blanket on a bed and a blackened teapot, there is hardly any other furniture in the room.

I recall that her house was not too far from the elementary school I attended. At that time her family was relatively well off and I would often sneak out in between classes to her house. There I could always find the best food, like tsampa and butter, to fill my ever-hungry stomach, and she had always generously offered me her best, never acting stingy.

Now at ninety-one, she has as her caretaker her son, who is in his fifties. Although her dwelling is dilapidated and miserable, she still maintains a cheerful disposition. She spouted funny tales she had heard from different sources, and we could not stop laughing. Lastly, she said: "I must have committed some evil deeds in past lives that I suffer this illness now, and I can only pray to the Three Jewels faithfully to lighten my karmic retributions."

Hearing her remarks, I saw the reason for her cheerful disposition. Her belief in the effects of positive and negative actions is firm enough that even when stricken with severe illness, she bears no grudges toward fate or others. Instead, she prays to the Three Jewels wholeheartedly and performs the purification practice guilelessly. No wonder she can remain composed. Indeed, anyone confident in the principle of cause and effect will always maintain a sunny outlook, even amid the most challenging circumstances.

July 17

My Alma Mater

THE THUNDERSTORM that raged all night finally stopped, and now the sun smiles from behind the clouds. In the washed, transparent air, the green fields are simply enchanting. The brooks run gently, nourishing Zong Ta prairie surrounded by verdant mountains and dense forests, while up above, white and golden swans glide gracefully in the sky. Bees and butterflies dance merrily among the sprawling white wildflowers and frogs leap playfully in tall grasses.

I am revisiting the spot where my alma mater, Zong Ta Middle School, used to be. An elementary school has replaced the old, ruined classrooms, and the dormitory I used to stay in is now a newly built bungalow. The lovely middle school days flash through my mind like scenes in a movie. In those days, we were bubbling over with vigor as if loaded with inexhaustible energy. And now, deserted by youth, I have only a sack of pale flesh and bones left, and many of my teachers have passed away. The saplings we planted around the campus are now towering trees adorned with luxuriant leaves, but many classmates who helped are heard no more and nowhere found. Standing on the hill overlooking my old school, I am choked with emotion; as things change, so do humans, only worse. Impermanence, like an iron-faced umpire, swallows up all there was in the past. It allows us no clinging to what we have now. It forces us to see the fleeting nature of the dreamy landscape and the composite human body.

But there is also something to be joyous about. My classmate Lhapu has taken the Buddhist ordination and is now the head monk of a monastery on a facing mountain, teaching Dharma to forty to fifty monks every day. Thinking of him makes me catch a glimpse of the everlasting beacon amid the rubble of impermanence.

July 18

Dhomang Monastery

THE MONKS of Dhomang Monastery have invited me to visit, so I went to give a talk today. At the risk of saying nothing new, I shared my concerns with the sanghas. Dhomang Monastery has always been cared for by eminent masters who have upheld pure precepts, such as the current Khenpo Depa, who is now at a ripe old age. Although the monastery thrives and has trained many learned khenpos, there is a gap between the old and young generations. The need for young and able leaders who can really take the baton and run with it cannot be more urgent.

As members of the monastic order, we have on our shoulders the critical mission of ensuring its survival and transmission. We must maintain a great aspiration and an open mind, steering our course steadily without being swept away. The comfort of this life is not what we are after. Instead, we should rival one another on possessing wisdom and compassion rather than wardrobes or mansions. A Gelug master once said: "Without renouncing the mundane world, all the study, contemplation, and meditation are but semblances of the real thing and entirely meaningless."

I left each of them a copy of *Jewel Garland from a Mountain Hermitage* by Tulku Zagar as a gift. I sincerely hope that by following our predecessor's footsteps, they will find inner peace and joy based on learning and meditation. Even though I did not talk to many of the sangha members in person, I feel a kinship with them, as we are all monks who have renounced the world to seek liberation. I am glad to share the experiences I gained while trudging along the spiritual path. An authentic practitioner must accept loneliness willingly and be free from never-ending worldly involvement. How can one talk about renunciation without giving up indulgence in sensual pleasures? What can be said about liberating others when one has not yet liberated oneself? Do not be trapped by lust, hatred, and delusion anymore! Think thrice! Think thrice!

July 19

Consecration Ceremony

DHOMANG MONASTERY holds a consecration ceremony today (June 11 in the Tibetan calendar) for its newly finished stupa of Shakyamuni Buddha. At the same time, the annual Offering to Dharma Protectors falls today and on the thirteenth. Dressed in festival outfits and riding their horses, people from the nine villages of greater Lekhogma village congregate on the prairie of Zuo Dang. The grassland over a radius of two kilometers is full of various kinds of tents.

The Ke Luo River ripples and sparkles brilliantly like shining jewels under the full sun. The lush greenery of the mountains resembles brocade draperies, and birds sing in the woods, their melodious tones rivaling celestial music. Forty years ago, such an exquisite, heavenly environment attracted me when I could hardly wait to emerge from my mother's womb and arrive in this world. Soon, aromatic smoke from burnt cypress branches spirals up into the sky. Men holding the flags of Dharma protectors (*lungtas*) perform circumambulations while tossing the lungtas toward the sky, making the whole prairie an ocean of colorful flags. In a huge tent accommodating up to a thousand people, many men again take an oath to refrain from drinking and killing. Many took the same vow last year, bringing impressive results. In the past year, there were hardly any cases of indiscriminate killing of the innocent, and people have come to see drinking and taking lives as shameful, thus reducing plenty of bad karma in a place once infamous for yak-meat production.

As the bloody atmosphere of the past has abated, the air seems more refreshing and pristine. The river, no longer running with the blood of sheep or yaks, appears more limpid and cooler. The pretty field, free from the distant wails of animals, feels more peaceful. If I were looking for a birthplace again, I would undoubtedly pick this place, as I am deeply in love with this land full of people blessed with kind and tender hearts.

July 20

A Dilemma

EVEN THE MOST knowledgeable and learned people will inevitably encounter dilemmas, let alone a person of shallow wisdom like me! An incident today threw me into a quandary.

A few days ago a lay practitioner, traveling far from the northeastern part of the country, visited me. He implored: "Lama, I have been reading your translation of *The Great Biography of Shakyamuni Buddha, the White Lotus*. The stories of the Buddha's aspirations and practices on his bodhisattva path struck me to the core. I yearn strongly to follow his example and renounce all worldly affairs to practice the way of enlightenment. Here I see thousands of Larung sangha members living a wholesome and unfettered life. How I wish to join them! I will drift and waste my life meaninglessly if I remain in the mundane world. Venerable Lama, please grant me my wishes!"

His sincerity touched me deeply, and I blessed him to become a monk. Then out of the blue, I received a call from his wife, who pleaded over the phone: "Venerable Khenpo! I am a devout Buddhist and wish for an ordained life free from worldly strife. But in our household, we have a son merely seven months old, a bedridden mother in the hospital, and I am without a job. Should my husband leave us, how does he expect his wife and orphaned son to survive? Is it proper for a Mahayana practitioner to abandon his ailing old mother, infant son, and helpless wife? Can he disregard their welfare and hide among the deep mountains to arouse bodhichitta?"

After hearing her side of the story, I was at a loss. The situation reminded me of a poem by His Holiness the Sixth Dalai Lama Tsang-yang Gyatso:

> I worried that being romantic would ruin my pure conduct,
> yet up in the mountains I felt vexed over losing my pretty lady.
> Why can't I have the best of both worlds
> that pleases the Tathagata and my sweetheart?

How can I find a perfect solution that will make everybody happy—in one way, find support for the lonely and desperate wife, and in another, fulfill her husband's wish of becoming a monk?

July 21

Being Ridiculed

APRACTITIONER'S DECISION to leave home on a spiritual retreat is often greeted with suspicion and mockery from worldly folks. But we should take this kind of ridicule and humiliation as supportive factors. All obstacles are but presages of accomplishment.

When the Tibetan Geshe Yulungpa was going into solitary retreat, one of his disciples tugged his robe and insistently asked for an essential instruction. The geshe replied earnestly: "Young man, although you have been a monk since an early age, it is still essential for you to see through the world's vanities. Always be humble and be content with just enough food to eat and enough clothes to keep warm. Take in your teacher's instruction like a thirsty person who gets to drink sweet spring water. Never turn back on the path, even if others insult you. Put all trivialities out of your mind and endeavor to practice persistently. By so doing, you cannot help but achieve success."

Geshe Potowa also says: "When others start feeling sorry for you, you should feel happy." In other words, when you have learned to swallow your pride and shun vanity, you will feel joyful when pitied by others. When you have personally experienced the bliss of practice, all external affairs lose their strong hold on you.

When Jetsun Mila was doing ascetic practices in a cave, several young women dropped in and could not help making pitying and sneering remarks. To them, Milarepa sang a song:

Unfortunate girls, you have faith only in ordinary life.
Your self-esteem and wrong perceptions burn like fire.
I feel pity for such immature beings.
You proud, pretty young girls and
I, Milarepa of Gungthang,
we see each other as pitiful:
you feel sorry for me, and I feel for you.
Let us compare and see who's going to win.
To those ignorant ones indulging in idle talk,
Milarepa replies by teaching the Dharma.
He returns rare jade for hard stone,
he returns fine wine for plain water.

Hence, people are most pitiful when they don't have the right view and are ignorant. How could others' foolish taunting shake our conviction in Dharma practice? It instead arouses our great compassion for them, to say the least.

July 22

Cultivating Selflessness

THE URGE to survive is a universal wish of all humans living under the same sky. One's life purpose, however, varies tremendously from person to person. For someone of high morals, to live means to benefit many other people. For ordinary folks, it means to care for themselves and their circle of family and friends. A small-minded person will unsparingly work day and night only on what he cherishes: his self-interests.

· Usually, relinquishing the selfish mind is next to impossible, whether one is the most learned, the smartest, the most knowledgeable, or has studied the sayings of many sages. Since time long past, we have been living for our own welfare. This intractable habitual pattern can only be cast off by extremely tenacious effort on our part. That is, we must start working in bits and pieces and persist with an unrelenting resolve akin to wearing down a rock with water droplets.

The collection *Living with Himalayan Masters* has this story: Little lama Tsondru practiced with his master. They ate only one meal a day at noon, so lunchtime became his happiest hour of the day. One day his master told him: "We have an eminent old monk visiting us today; you should offer your food to him."

"I can't do it! I get hungry too. Even if the visitor is a monk, he should not deprive me of my right to eat, and this tiny amount of food is the only meal I have for today."

"You will not die from starvation. Let him have your food!"

"But my stomach is rumbling!"

"You must!"

As it turned out, the young monk's relished lunch became someone else's enjoyment. But from then on, he learned to be unselfish, and offering became easy for him, even if it meant giving away his most-cherished belongings. He finally came to see the wisdom of his master in urging him to surrender his food. In giving up the possessions he clung to, he gained entry to the vast arena of selflessness.

Once, Buddha Shakyamuni met a little beggar who only said "I want it, I want it" all the time. The Buddha first made the beggar say "I do not want it, I do not want it," and then rewarded him with food. In this way, the Buddha planted the seed of generosity in the beggar's mind. We should follow the adage to eliminate our deep-rooted habit of self-ishness: "Do not fail to do any good deeds, no matter how insignificant they may seem"—starting by letting go of one penny, one bowl of rice, or one yard of fabric.

July 23

Taking Refuge

MANY PEOPLE have taken refuge in the Three Jewels, yet their motivation varies enormously. Entering the gate of Buddhism is like walking into a big supermarket fully stocked with all kinds of goods to satisfy everyone's needs and likes. Some take refuge in the idea of obtaining the happiness of gods and men, and others are motivated by the fear of the lower realms. Some take refuge in the Three Jewels to attain freedom from samsaric sufferings, while others do so hoping to liberate all sentient beings. The first three attitudes are those of lesser- and middling-capacity beings; only the last one is the supreme motivation of great beings. To take refuge solely for selfish desire is like trading a wish-fulfilling jewel for a piece of candy—very shortsighted indeed. When farmers grow rice, they expect to reap rice grains, but at the same time hay will automatically become available to them too. Likewise, if a person works wholeheartedly for other sentient beings without any egoistic concern, his own liberation will come naturally, even without asking for it.

The omniscient Longchenpa left a concise sadhana for taking refuge. We first make offerings and confessions before the Three Jewels' representations. Visualize the Buddha, Dharma, Sanghas, and other deities filling the sky before you. Make cloud-like outer, inner, and secret offerings to them, and say: "From this time until attaining the essence of enlightenment, I [say your name], for the sake of all sentient beings, take refuge in the Buddha. I take refuge in the Dharma. I take refuge in the Sangha." Say this three times from the depths of your heart, and with the help of symbols (the teacher snapping his fingers or your own imagining), the refuge vow is attained.

This ritual is simple and significant. Some Dharma instructors among you may have guided others to take refuge in the past without following a sadhana. Consider using this text for the ritual of taking refuge. I sometimes did not use a sadhana and will adhere to this text closely in the future.

July 24

Feeling Lonesome

AFTER LUNCH, I went off to close my door as usual. Seeing this, the lama next door asked me quizzically: "You lock yourself up in your room every afternoon. Don't you ever feel lonely?" "Not at all. I find great pleasure in it!"

I was telling the truth. Each day, through reading books, I communicate intimately with many sages and great masters; through insight meditation, I get along well with friends of innate wisdom. It is much better than idling away time in chatter or fruitlessly sightseeing. What's more, if I were not careful about what to adopt and what to avoid, I might hang out with scoundrels who incite greediness, hatred, and delusion. Wouldn't I be a raving fool if I committed evil acts due to my foolish choice? Consider this adage:

> Associating with a man of noble character, you will be influ-
> enced positively over time without knowing it yourself.
> Associating with a man of mean character is like walking on
> thin ice. How can you avoid falling into misery?

Associating with a noble-minded person, we can't help being influenced positively over time. On the other hand, keeping company with an evil person is like being led onto thin ice: we will find ourselves falling into dangerous icy waters and becoming defiled. Great sages appearing in this world are few and far between; they are our jewel-like, best counsel. How can I let slip a chance to learn from them? Even if such noble characters with perfect wisdom lived today, would we have the heart to disturb them daily and waste their precious time? By being alone, I have come to appreciate its immense beauty profoundly.

My happiest hour of the day is when I can talk heart-to-heart with great sages of the past behind closed doors and drawn curtains. In the guise of being away from home, I have intimate chats with friends of awareness.

If I could not stand being lonely and instead searched for worldly companions or traveled about, would that be helpful at all? A practitioner once told me: If your heart is lonely, that feeling is there even when you are mingling with a big crowd. If your heart is not lonely, you are happy even spending your life alone in a cave. Loneliness comes from the heart.

The Precious Treasury of Pith Instructions has many insightful teachings on this topic. Our loneliness is self-inflicted and not changeable by manipulating external conditions. If you understand this, would you still consider going places to rid yourself of loneliness?

July 25

A Shepherd Boy

THE FREEZING SEASON, when we can see our condensed breath, has arrived quietly. Thick frost covers the grass in the morning, and the fields soon become parched, brittle, and brown. As I was about to leave the house for the day, I came across a shepherd boy of about fifteen or sixteen in worn-out clothes. He walked barefoot and held a mala in one hand. This figure is strikingly similar to my own some twenty years ago.

Although the calendar on the wall indicates the world is now in the twenty-first century, the march of time has stalled in this remote highland region, where the shepherd boy today still does not own a pair of shoes. I knew only too well those painful stings of walking barefoot on brittle autumn grasses. How I wished to own a pair of shoes then! I remember my father finally got me a new pair of rubber shoes. However, perhaps due to my lack of merit, the boots were too small, and wearing them tortured my feet. Afraid of losing the new shoes I had yearned for so long, I bore the agonizing pain and dared to take them off to relieve my sore feet briefly only when no one was around.

We were so poor in material possessions in those years, yet we were rich in the most valuable thing spiritually—loving-kindness. Seeing the sufferings of other creatures—little ants on the brink of being drowned, earthworms exposed to the scorching sun, fish in a pond running dry of water—we would feel the same pain as they did and try to rescue them from danger.

Isn't it fortunate to have such a childhood? Other children may lead a sheltered life, with parents who wear designer outfits, live in a mansion, drive deluxe cars, and feast on seafood dishes. But the children's innate compassion and loving-kindness are smothered by what they learn from their parents. Compared with them, am I not luckier a thousand times over and beyond?

Seeing this shepherd boy with a mala in hand, I do not doubt that he, like my boyhood friends, must have a heart bejeweled with kindness. I invited him to my place and offered him candies and fruit. Although I did not have a suitable pair of shoes for him, I could see from his eyes that he was already quite happy. He bid goodbye to me cheerfully and ran fast to catch his yak, already quite a distance away.

July 26

Magic Power

A DHARMA FRIEND CONFIDED his recent experiences to me: "A while ago, I was besieged by all kinds of problems. Because of heavy obscurations and my lack of self-cultivation, I responded vehemently with self-attachment. I saw that I was falling into a pit of my own digging, but I had no way to extricate myself. My troubled emotions went haywire to such an extent that I even contemplated suicide.

"As a Buddhist, I knew too well that I should not choose a track that is tantamount to an abyss. When Milarepa was about to kill himself, Lama Ngokpa restrained him and said: 'The faculties and the senses of each of us are innately divine. If you die before your time, even by the transference of consciousness, you commit the sin of killing a buddha.' Moreover, our mind is primordially pure; only the confused emotions prompted by circumstances cause us to suffer. How can I take the illusory appearance as real and true? Again and again, I tried to console myself. Yet as evil karma played out unstoppably, I was crushed by a piercing pain that I can never forget.

"One day, I dragged my heavy legs to the window and saw crowds busily coming and going on the street, all striving for food, clothes, fame, and money. Suddenly I realized how lucky I was! They are oblivious that their ignorance and delusion will lead to lower realms; in contrast, I have in my hand the supreme instruction for gaining liberation in this very life.

"Although I am not yet free from suffering, at least I can carefully choose what to do and what to avoid, thus minimizing the causes of future suffering. And trying my best to recognize the nature of suffering, I can say that liberation is not too far away. My suffering amounts to nothing compared to that of many others who still face endless miseries. Repeatedly, before the Three Jewels, I fervently pledged to liberate all sentient beings. Now, if I cannot break free from the narrow confines of the 'I,' all my vows are but actor's lines, pale and lifeless.

"I know that the only option to eliminate self-grasping is to pray to the guru and the Three Jewels, purify defilements, and arouse bodhichitta. After working hard for a while, I finally found my way out of the dark valley. And should obstacles arise again, I can handle them more skillfully.

"Making use of Buddha's teachings, I have become more resilient. As someone who has lived a sheltered life, the whole episode was a life lesson on the sufferings of samsara. By experiencing them personally, genuine renunciation has taken birth in me. This realization would not have dawned had I not been plagued by my afflictions in the first place. I thank the blessings of the Three Jewels that have rescued me from hindrances and pains. I have discovered the immense value of our human existence—to attain enlightenment for the benefit of all beings. This, and only this, is the goal I will strive for life after life!"

After hearing his story, I felt deeply gratified that he had overcome difficulties with vigilance and mindfulness. Whenever we are at our wits' end, mired in mundane affairs, it is time to apply the Buddha's teachings as antidotes. Such is the magical power of the Dharma.

July 27

To Soar

PEOPLE who have established some certainty about the Buddhist view will, upon careful analysis, come to perceive that all experiences—whether the mind is actively thinking or abiding in calmness, whether one is talking volubly or keeping a vow of silence, whether one is walking, standing, sitting, or sleeping, whether one is feeling happy, sad, bitter, or jealous—are illusory and insubstantial. And eventually it dawns on them that all displays, inner or outer, are inseparable from the wisdom of the dharmadhatu.

Those who have recognized the true face of the mind experience the dissolution of greed, hatred, and other defilements into awareness, similar to water dissolving into water. No longer subject to the whims of their emotions, they enjoy the great bliss of being free, not unlike a prisoner released from constricting shackles.

Regrettably, worldly beings remain ignorant of this truth. They tightly grasp the ropes of greed and enmity and endure immense suffering as a result. As an antidote, Longchenpa says:

> From time to time, consider your own and others' physical actions; you will feel that they have no true existence, seeing them as you would those of dancers giving a performance.
>
> From time to time, consider the sounds we utter when we speak; you will find them ineffable, the unity of sound and emptiness, and so perceive them as you would an echo.
>
> From time to time, consider whatever arises in your mind,

whether pleasant or painful; you will see it as the display of awareness, and so experience the way things actually are.

From time to time, consider the very essence of thought, of what stirs and is recalled in the mind; you will experience the natural dissolution of ordinary consciousness and perceive dharmakaya in all its immediacy.

From time to time, consider the unwavering state of mind itself; you will experience enlightened intent, in which everything resolves, and so perceive that there is no proliferation and subsiding of thought.

From time to time, consider the imperturbable state of rest, free of any conscious striving; you will see that nothing need be done, and so a sense of ease will permeate your being.*

Like the dazzling sun, the teachings of great Nyingma masters dispel the mist of ignorance and illuminate a thoroughfare to liberation. If we practice accordingly, we will recognize the truth of suffering and penetrate our inner radiance. Soon we will be in the company of awareness holders, the Vidyadharas, and our tender and immature wings of wisdom and compassion will grow strong and become fully fledged. Then, soaring freely in the clear expanse of the dharmakaya like a golden-winged garuda, we fly straight to the Pure Land of Buddha Samantabhadra.

These wish-granting jewels are right next to us all the time. Have we noticed them and made good use of them?

July 28

---

* Longchen Rapjam, *The Precious Treasury of Pith Instructions*, trans. Richard Barron (Padma Publishing, 2006), 148–49.

An Old Nun

LOOKING OUT the reception room window, I saw an old Tibetan nun at the end of a long line reverently doing prostrations. Her robe was soiled, she had a bundle of grimy vajra cords with insignias around her neck, her calloused left hand held a mala tied with numerous tiny knots, and layers of heavy dust masked her graying hair. Her face was covered with bumps and marred by countless wrinkles. At the corner of her mouth, some leftover tsampa, either from this morning or the previous day, came loose as she murmured prayers. The holes in her socks exposed big toes with long, dark toenails, and a pair of black shoes sat stiffly by her side. The only lively parts of her body were the pink tip of her wiggling tongue and her bloodshot eyes.

Noticing my smile to her, she grinned, revealing dark brown teeth, and limped toward me. In a hoarse and slurred voice, she told me she was from Qinghai Province and that her husband had long since passed away. Her four sons, whom she had raised in considerable hardship, ignored her spitefully. Having nowhere to turn, she came to Larung about three years ago. In this harmonious big family, she no longer fears being ridiculed or deserted and is living happily through the blessings of the gurus.

I asked her: "Your sons have mistreated you; do you hate them?" She replied calmly: "This is the payback for my previous evils and I have nothing to blame. I can only pray to the buddhas, bodhisattvas, and teachers and purify my own karma. There are so many accomplished beings at Larung. Even if I were to die today, I would have no fear, as by the power of all the blessings bestowed on me, I will certainly be reborn in the Pure Land of Great Bliss."

Her unshakable and unquestionable faith touched me deeply. What a precious jewel hid beneath her smudged appearance! She has resolved to face life with a smile. Her words about her indomitable faith toward lineage masters and the Three Jewels far surpassed the high-sounding opinions and debates of the young and aggressive. Moreover, she outshined the well-dressed worldly gentry.

Just then, someone offered me a tray of hot, steaming buns, and I immediately passed them to her. She happily received them and hurriedly said thank you: "Khatro! Khatro!" She then took her leave while continuing to chant the mantra of Avalokiteshvara and turn the prayer wheel. Gazing at her receding figure, I prayed wholeheartedly for her and all older people to live their twilight years joyfully.

July 29

Without Regret

THE NAME Lama Gracho is greatly renowned throughout Larung Buddhist Academy, where he has conferred empowerments and transmitted the terma revealed by Rigdzin Godkyi Demtruchen. For our Guru Jigme Phuntsok Rinpoche, he wrote the long-life prayer that everyone at Larung has faithfully recited.

He made his first pilgrimage to Jokhang Temple in Lhasa in his youth. As witnessed by his travel companions, while he prostrated to pay homage to the statue of Jowo Shakyamuni, a bright light streamed from the Buddha's heart to his heart, and he passed out on the spot. When he came to, the realization of the primordial dharmakaya wisdom arose in him. Henceforth he devoted his entire life to the Dharma.

His leg became crippled during the Cultural Revolution, which spared him the torture of incarceration. He fasted long term while practicing in his tent, where unseasonal grass shoots appeared even during the most severe winter blizzard conditions. When subjected to public political persecution, he vowed that for the benefit of all beings, he would train himself in forbearance. When he was beaten or kicked ruthlessly by rebel factions, he bore not a shred of hatred but remained in a state beyond all artifice and contrivance. At the end of his persecution, he dedicated his merit entirely to all beings, his tormentors foremost among them.

When the calamity came to an end, his crippled leg miraculously healed. Although the world tried hard to woo him with its lures, he remained unmoved and untarnished by the eight mundane concerns.

He immersed himself in meditation until entering nirvana at 6:30 pm on February 27, 2000.

Two days before entering nirvana, he told his disciples: "From a young age until now, I have engaged in mundane affairs as well as the Dharma. At times I chased after fame, holding low positions or high posts. Now my end is near. When facing death, nothing is helpful except practicing the exchange of oneself with others. You should all earnestly pray to Guru Padmasambhava, the sovereign of this degenerate time. Observe the law of causality vigilantly as if guarding your own life. Focus on one practice so that you'll have no regrets when dying. I have no more to say at this last hour. Please arrange magnificent offerings!" Thus said, he prayed unceasingly to Guru Padmasambhava until he passed away.

At the commencement of the cremation ceremony his body appeared much younger and many people witnessed his appearance as the white Vajrasattva, which aroused tremendous faith in everyone.

Numerous adept practitioners like him have devoted their lives to the Dharma. When encountering adversity, they do not complain or feel sorry for themselves but rather persevere in meditation. Finally, they leave this world while resting in the great bliss of primordial wisdom.

As for us self-proclaimed practitioners, on the deathbed will we also be free from enmity and regret when looking back on our lives?

July 30

Dharma Bliss

TODAY at Larung Academy, we are all overjoyed that our loving guru, Jigme Phuntsok Rinpoche, is resuming his teaching paused since last summer due to his illness. This occasion means that our guru has regained his health to some degree, allowing him to shower us with the Dharma nectar.

Rinpoche has chosen to teach the *Sutra of the Wise and the Foolish*. He says he has been giving Dharma teachings for many decades, since his teens. It would be a piece of cake to teach the great five major treatises or transmit the secret Mantrayana, even with his failing eyesight. But in the current degenerate time and materialistic society, many people, Buddhists included, neglect the infallible karmic law and the sufferings of samsara; they cater to misdeeds and forget the ominous afterlife awaiting them. Thus, he feels that teaching the *Sutra of the Wise and the Foolish* is imperative and relevant, to warn disciples to give up evils and accept causality. The stories in this sutra are not to be read as fables; instead, they are the Conqueror's adamantine words imbued with profound meaning. Their power to tame destructive emotions and confer benefit to all is inconceivable.

I am privileged to serve as a translator for this teaching. Hearing our master's voice, we are transported through time and space back to the good old days, and our eyes brim with tears. I felt a lump in my throat a few times. Indeed, we are all thirsting intensely for the Dharma, and once we have been immersed in the Dharma bliss, how can we not weep with joy?

July 31

Lion's Fortress

HE LION'S FORTRESS is the sacred place where our Guru Jigme Phuntsok Rinpoche studied and taught the *Seven Treasures* in his youth. I have always wanted to visit it, but my yearning remained unfulfilled until today. After lunch, Tsultrim Lodro, Chime Rigdzin, and I decided to make a pilgrimage to the sacred Ala Mountain. Shortly after leaving Larung Valley, we came upon a water reservoir with three stupas nearby. Tsultrim Lodro said: "I am getting tired and would like to nap on this hillside. You two continue." Obliging, Chime Rigdzin and I began to scale the mountain along the ridge, through which ran a limpid brook. Pine trees on the sunny side of the watershed and cypresses on the shady side greeted each other across the distance. The intense sun shone directly on us, and my back was wet with sweat in no time.

We then walked into a deep forest where towering trees, dense with growth that blocked the sun, made it dim and hampered our view. We made high-pitched sounds to steel ourselves and warn the mountain bears about our presence. At last we arrived at our destination, where we were immediately captivated by a wealth of amazing views. It was indeed worth the trip! There were white and reddish rocks, some shaped like lions, others like forts, and some like a pile of scriptures. Perhaps that's how the name Lion's Fortress came about. A profusion of blooming flowers in the fields dazzled our eyes, and the wild fruit on the tree branches whetted our appetites.

The remains of the hut where our teacher used to stay were still clearly visible, even after forty years. Chime Rigdzin and I made three prostrations to the hut and started to recite the *Aspiration of the Great Perfection*. Finishing the recitation, I asked Chime Rigdzin, "Isn't this place, with its crystal-clear brook and abundant wild fruit, a perfect place for a retreat? We should retire here to practice in our later years." He answered: "Why wait until then? It's not impossible to do it now." Recalling how often Patrul Rinpoche and Longchenpa praised secluded places, we sighed deeply. It would be most desirable if we could cut off all worldly concerns and live here for our remaining years, far away from bustling mundane life!

Before we knew it, the sun was setting, and Chime Rigdzin and I had no choice but to reluctantly leave. We then met up with Tsultrim Lodro, who, having anxiously awaited our return, said: "I have been waiting so long for you!" Chime Rigdzin and I exchanged a knowing smile, thinking of our secret pleasure. There's a saying, "Playing a game of chess in heaven, thousands of earthly years passed." Through the power of the sacred mountain's blessing, we had been transported to another era and lost track of time. Tsultrim Lodro should be content that he had not waited for thousands of years!

You may be curious and ask how to get to this wonderland. I'll tell you, climb up near the three stupas next to the water reservoir. Go straight up, and you'll get there. Try it, you are bound to enjoy a refreshing experience!

August 3

Dharma Protectors

TODAY marks the annual Protector's Day at Larung Buddhist Academy. According to legend, the First Dudjom Rinpoche once had a dispute with Goddess Mutian, the guardian of the western mountain, and drove her out to the Luhuo area. Through the mediation of a great master, the two parties reached an agreement. Every year on June 26 of the Tibetan calendar (the day the goddess returns to Larung), the disciples of Dudjom Rinpoche's lineage are to make an offering ceremony to the protectors. The Goddess Mutian is to occupy the head of the protectors, and no more troublemaking is allowed from her. This observation has continued without interruption for nearly twenty years.

At eight in the morning, thousands of sangha members holding colorful banners climb Larung's Wutai Mountain in an area corresponding to the individual's designated residence. A few years ago, H. H. Jigme Phuntsok Rinpoche consecrated Larung's Wutai Mountain when he invoked the presence of the buddhas and bodhisattvas of Tibet's five sacred mountains and those of Han China's Wutai Mountain. It then earned the title "Wutai Mountain of Tibet," endowed with extraordinary blessings.

As I have always been interested in making offerings to the protectors, I make the trip today to the eastern region of the mountaintop (my designated residence, Mani Jewel Land) in high spirits despite my lingering back pain. At nine o'clock, sangha members on five peaks start their sadhana recitations and the offering of burning cypress branches. Five streams of smoke, like five khatas, spiral upward and join in the sky to form a puffy white cloud sailing in the blue sky. The expansive space, like the face of a pretty maiden, is made more charming by the gorgeous adornment of clouds. The red monk's robes are like crimson corals floating in the green fields, prayer flags swirling in the air resemble a rain of flowers scattered by goddesses, and the snow peaks of the surrounding mountains sparkle like jewels. I feel like I'm in a vast mandala, and I make offerings of body, speech, and mind in unison with the sangha members to the sacred deities in ten directions. This practice will alleviate all hostile forces and accomplish all positive qualities and activities, worldly and spiritual.

Today is a rare occasion for sangha members to relax and take a break. In the afternoon, they sit in small groups on the lawn and enjoy the warm sunshine. While the breeze gently caresses them, they take in the fragrance of flowers and listen to the whispering of worms. Their faces beam with radiant smiles, and the entire troop of protectors must be delighted now!

August 4

Banishing Self-Centeredness

THIS MORNING I spent an hour receiving visitors from various places and backgrounds. Many topics are touched on, but regrettably, almost all of them revolve around "I"—my problems, my family, my spiritual training, my teacher, my desire for liberation, and my wish for accomplishment. In short, that's all there is.

Why can't we escape from the control of the "I"? From time without beginning, we have paid dearly for this singular "I." Like an invisible lasso, it makes us live in self-confinement and intoxication—we always feel uneasy because of our constant worry about gain and loss. *Entering the Middle Way* says:

> Initially fixating on this so-called I as an existing self,
> "mine" gives rise to grasping.
> Helpless beings, driven like an irrigation wheel. . .

Driven by habits due to ignorance, sentient beings mistakenly take the composite "I" of the four elements as truly existing, fueling the grip on "I" and "mine." Grasping leads to afflictions, and afflictions to misdeeds, resulting in samsaric cycling without end.

If the "I" assumes command of your being, analyze its true face meticulously until you discover that the physical body and the mind are illusory, not having the tiniest bit of reality. How can outer circumstances inflict trouble on us if our body and mind do not truly exist? Meditating in this way, clinging to the "I" and "mine" will gradually diminish and finally disappear altogether, along with afflictive emotions.

We are now sailing in the vast ocean toward liberation. Beware the underwater reefs of the "I," lest we cast down heavy anchors and stall our spiritual journey.

August 5

Words and Conduct

THERE GOES the sharp pain torturing my poor back again. I can't help groaning and lamenting to the little lama beside me: "What shall I do? It hurts so much!" He replied: "But haven't you told us that in sickness, we should visualize exchanging ourselves with others and take their sufferings upon ourselves? Isn't this the way to diminish self-attachment and relieve pain?"

The little lama's words leave me so embarrassed that I could have sunk through the floor. How often have I sat on high podiums and prattled on and on, admonishing others with lofty principles: "We must transform adversity and illness into spiritual growth!" Then I seem to toss these words away irresponsibly, without disciplining myself accordingly. Wouldn't I be fittingly described as "a giant in words, a dwarf in action?"

Examining my recent conduct, I see that in the face of difficulties I care greatly about my mood swings and sorrows; this obstinate self-grasping tends to get the upper hand. But don't I know that the three realms are but a house on fire? So how can there be no suffering? As an ordinary being, the imbalance of the four elements is expected, so why should I make a big deal out of my illness? And why should I become frustrated to no avail? Sickness is the best time to practice the Dharma! Reviewing these lines of reasoning, I scold myself and work on exchanging myself with others. The result, I feel, is quite good.

I use a microscope to find fault with others while revealing nothing about my defects. What the little lama says is enlightening, and I see my flaws that are otherwise difficult to spot. An ancient adage goes: "When put into action, even one piece of good advice brings lifetime benefit. When not put into action, even all the books in the world offer no benefit whatsoever." Therefore, I must walk the talk in my daily life. Otherwise, I'll be like a fool who dies from thirst in front of water.

August 6

Mountain Hare

TIBETANS usually praise the mountain hare as a "bodhisattva." Our native species sports a white belly and black back, two big eyes, and a pair of big, floppy ears. They have a very gentle and loving disposition.

A few months ago, a mountain hare decided to make its home in a pine tree in my yard and has become my new neighbor. Every day while the sun is still snuggling in bed, my diligent neighbor has already filled his belly with dew-laden grass and returned home to assume his "meditation." He remains motionless all morning, working skillfully on "looking at the vajra chains" and "looking into the void," just like an old-hand yogi.

The hare does not leave his "meditation cell" until it's time to nibble tender grasses again in the afternoon. As we are getting along well, he considers me one of his kind and does not bother establishing any protective measures. Even if I walk past his "meditation cell," he couldn't care less and will not blink an eye.

With a kind heart, the hare never harms other beings. Compared with urban folks who ooze foul odors from feasting on seafood or slurping live monkey brains, the hare lives a pure and unfettered life. How I love having him as a neighbor! A song of realization declares: "In the clear sky the moon shines alone; under the towering pine trees the mountain hare sits alone; spiritual seeker in the deep forest, you are never alone." I rejoice in the carefree solitude enjoyed by the hare!

The sun lowers its curtain for the day, and the night sky will soon take the stage. It's time for the hare to return to his burrow and for me to turn on the light to resume my daily homework.

August 7

A Palmful of Water

T HIS STORY is told in the *Sutra of the Wise and Foolish*: A lay practitioner who observed the five precepts once led five hundred mer-
chants on a journey in search of precious gems in the ocean. A sea god,
exercising his magic powers, tried to impede them. The captain took
the opportunity to teach the sea god by enumerating the sufferings
of hell and the preta realm, and the noble deeds of virtuous people.
When the sea god's arrogance finally dissipated, he filled his palm with
water and said: "Lay disciple, tell me, which is greater, the water in my
palm or the water in the sea?" The captain answered: "The water in
your palm is greater." The sea god asked, "Are you sure?" The captain
replied, "What I say is true and I do not err. Although the ocean water is
vast, as the present kalpa draws closer to the time of destruction, seven
suns will arise in the sky, whence Mount Meru will burn up and none of
the water in the seven oceans will remain. On the other hand, whoever
offers even a palmful of water to the Buddha, the sangha, one's parents,
the poor, and animals will gain indestructible virtue throughout the
kalpas. For this reason, the water in your palm is more significant than
all the water in the sea." The sea god was elated. He took out his treasures, presented them to the captain, and entrusted him to send many
exquisite gems to the Buddha and monks.

When we look at the boundless ocean, we marvel at its limitless
expanse but never imagine it will dry up one day. This story about one
palmful of water reminds us that any positive action done with wisdom
and skillful means will lead to incredible results. Every morning, after

washing up, we shall remember to offer a cup of clean water at the shrine with a pure mind. Through the power of excellent offering, this little cup of water surpasses even the seven oceans in bringing about merit. Won't you give it a try joyfully?

August 8

Devastating News

I GOT SOME terrible news: An acquaintance named Sangye Rangpo died tragically and his corpse was brought over to Larung today. He was a handsome guy, tall and heavyset. He used to carry a longsword at the girdle and loved to gallop over the prairie on fine horses. He knew how to hold himself during scuffles and took pride in his fighting skills. I met him not too long ago at Dhomang Monastery, and I asked him: "What use is it to you to carry this long sword? Wouldn't you be just fine without it?" But he vehemently defended doing so. Little did I know that it would be the last time we would see each other.

A few days ago, he started a fight with someone over a trivial matter and was stabbed in the chest by his opponent. He managed to utter only a few words: "You have killed me!" before spitting up blood and dying. A young life full of vigor and vitality thus ended so abruptly, in less than a few minutes. The sharp knife pierced through his chest, splattering scarlet blood over the green pasture, and the wails of his family reached the clouds. When police arrived at the scene, the villain had long since dashed away. Enraged by the murder, Sangye's younger brother set fire to the perpetrator's tent and burned it down. But a life lost can never be reclaimed. This feud between two families has just begun. When will the cycle of reprisal and retaliation come to an end?

Our life, more precious than gold and as fleeting as a water bubble, is to be cherished and made good use of. Yet many people, for the sake of coveting loved ones and fighting enemies, only engage in evil deeds. The *Sutra of the Wise and Foolish* says:

Warriors and generals, bold and fierce, charge into battlefields
and kill enemies with knives, swords, spearheads, and so
forth.
As retributions for these evils, they fall into terrible hells after
death and suffer long-lasting torments.

Worldly folks regard being daring and aggressive on the battlefield
as praiseworthy. Little do they realize that this is the cause of rebirth
in the hell realm. Anyone who ignores the consequences of actions is
utterly pathetic!

Now, I pray silently: Through the blessings of the Three Jewels, may
Sangye Rangpo turn away from the wrong path and be swiftly liberated from samsara. Lama chen!

August 9

Two Benefits

FOR AN ordinary person, the best way to benefit others is to cultivate love, compassion, and bodhichitta. Once bodhichitta is generated and sustained, one will not fall into the three lower realms. Even
if it's inevitable because of past evil karma, its duration will be as short
as the time it takes to snap one's fingers.

A layperson asked Dromtonpa: "Is the aspiration to uphold bodhichitta the direct or indirect cause of benefitting beings?" Dromtonpa
answered: "It is the best cause to benefit beings. One who embraces
bodhichitta will not fall into the lower realms but become a non-
returner. Even if some specific karma leads to rebirth into the lower
realms, one can still attain liberation at the instant of recalling bodhichitta, the power of which will propel one to the higher realms of
humans and gods."

However, avoiding the lower realms should not be the motivation
for performing virtues. Indeed, some self-styled Mahayanists may go
through the motions of arousing bodhichitta before practice and dedicating the merit at the end of practice sessions. By trying not to waste
their merit, they merely want to secure their own enlightenment and
happiness. Practice done in this way only disqualifies oneself as an
authentic Mahayana practitioner.

We should not vainly attempt to usurp bodhichitta for personal
gain, which only accomplishes the opposite. For eons, our excessive
self-interest has caused us to cycle in samsara endlessly. On the other
hand, buddhas and bodhisattvas have never cared about their own

interests, yet they attain the final fruition of buddhahood. Thus, the so-called two benefits enhance each other. A self-centered intention not only thwarts serving others but also entirely rules out self-benefit.

Therefore, before we do any virtuous actions, let's do a little soul searching: What kind of bodhichitta am I generating? Am I able to maintain a clear conscience? Do I really uphold the bodhisattva's vow in my mind?

August 10

Farewell Flowers

ONCE I MENTIONED my fondness for flowers in *The Sprays of the Wisdom Ocean*, flower gifts started to fill my house and garden. The China rose from Yuan Guan, the yellow chrysanthemum sent by Chime Tsultrim, and many others have turned my outdoor space into a grand spectacle of blooming flowers.

Even though I leave my house early in the morning, I always find time to water the flowers. Perhaps touched by my sincerity and tender care, they have repaid me with abundant gorgeous blossoms. With autumn in the air, my yard still maintains the glory of summer days. On my way home after class today, I notice the usually closed front gate is tilted ajar, and a gloomy foreboding comes up in me. Once in the yard, I am struck by the mess of scattered petals everywhere. A goat snores loudly among the fallen flowers, and a nearby pot holds its fresh excrement. Oh, you naughty fellow! My heart sinks as if I have lost my most cherished belonging. Burglars have raided my house many times, taking quite a few valuable items. Still, I didn't feel as bleak as I do over the lost flowers, a feeling I am perhaps predisposed to by having been a bee in my previous life.

Immediately this passage from the *Sutra Requested by Luoyan* springs up and bounces in front of me like a playful child. "A Mahabodhisattva should aspire thus: For the sake of beings, I would be willing to offer even my own body and flesh, not to mention my material possessions and other things." Suddenly my mind clears up. Amid the debris of the ravaged garden, my sadness dissipates like a vanishing fog and I feel a sense of relief, as if some heavy weight has been lifted from my heart and body.

My next-door lama suffers the same misfortune. Letting loose a torrent of abuse, he is ready to seek revenge with a rock in his hand. As a fellow victim, I appreciate how he feels. Nonetheless, I try to calm him down while pushing the goat to one corner so that at least the target of my neighbor's attack can be "out of sight, out of mind."

The garden, vibrant and luxuriant this morning, is now lifeless and messy, with red petals strewn all over. Isn't everything in the world just as ephemeral? Lama chen!

August 12

Pure Gold

PEOPLE USE gold as a metaphor for something precious, rare, and indestructible—for instance, we might say someone has "a heart of gold" or that "truth will prevail through fire just as genuine gold does." Gold accessories are also eye-catching. However, exterior ornamentation can do nothing for interior qualities. For that, one needs the Dharma. Sacred Dharma teachings can embellish one's present and future lives and ultimately bring liberation. Considering its limitless benefits, the value of the Dharma is as precious as the purest gold.

Dharma masters have bequeathed us legacies of pure gold. The foremost among them, Jowo Je Glorious Atisha, mastered all inner and outer doctrines by age twenty-one. He became proficient in sutras and tantras after diligent study under the formidable Naropa. Later, following the direction of his teachers and his yidam, Atisha took ordination from the supreme erudite Silarakshita and was given the name Dipamkara Srijnana. Within three years, he understood perfectly the essential points of his own and all other lineages.

Following his instruction from Tara, he took a perilous thirteen-month sea voyage and overcame unimaginable difficulties to arrive at the distant island of Sumatra, in present-day Indonesia. There, with deep and unshakable devotion, he studied and trained in bodhichitta for twelve years with the teacher he had long yearned for, Guru Suvarnadvipa, or the Master of Gold Isle. Having received his master's golden teachings, he aroused the golden bodhichitta and witnessed many pure visions of yidams. Atisha spoke of his guru with the greatest gratitude and would say with deep emotion: "The golden bodhichitta that I have generated in my mind all comes from the kindness of Lord Suvarnadvipa!"

Atisha returned to India fully accomplished. With his erudition and extraordinary wisdom, he triumphed in numerous heated debates against thirteen non-Buddhist extremists. He was offered thirteen victory banners from his defeated opponents, who were full of admiration and respect for him. His glorious fame spread far and wide. He won the total trust of the sangha at the eminent Buddhist Vikramashila Monastery and was entrusted with the stewardship of eighteen keys of the monastery. (In that period, to be in charge of merely one key was regarded as a great honor.)

The Tibetan king of that time, Lha Lama Yeshe O, gave up his life for an amount of gold equal to his body weight, which he would use to invite Atisha to Tibet. His nephew, Jangchup O, journeyed to India with this gold, offered it to Atisha, and brought the master to Tibet, where he taught the pure Dharma for thirteen years.

Once asked by his foremost disciples, Khu, Ngok, and Drom, to transmit the best elements of the path, Atisha replied with these illuminating words:

> The best instruction is always to direct all your practice
>   inward.
> The best conduct is one that does not conform to worldly ways.
> The best accomplishment is a steady lessening of afflictive
>   emotions.
> The best sign of practice is having less desire and knowing
>   contentment.
> The best spiritual friend is one who strikes your hidden faults.
> The best incentives for virtue are enemies, obstacles, and the
>   suffering of illness.

Great masters like Atisha have left us rich legacies like pure gold. If we travel to the golden isles only to return empty-handed, what could be more foolish?

August 14

Faith and Devotion

GENUINE DEVOTION is the root of attaining any spiritual accomplishment, great or small, especially for those engaged in tantric practice. If we always drench ourselves in kindness and reverence, we become receptive to the essence of Dharma. We must know that all the blessings of the mind lineage come from faith and devotion.

Should practitioners lack devotion and respect, they will never experience the state beyond words, even if they are brilliant and diligent, extremely capable, or have thoroughly read all the Tripitaka texts. It is only through incomparable and astounding devotion to their masters that many siddhas received mind-to-mind transmissions. Blessed by the peerless lineage, they realized the truth of dharmakaya, and they themselves became great lineage holders to guide beings and spread the Dharma far and wide. The biographies of great masters have vivid accounts of this marvelous process of Dharma transmission.

I know a person of average acumen who has made remarkable progress in his practice and achieved much. He told me once: "For a dull-witted person like me, only through faith and devotion to my guru and the Three Jewels can I attain any qualities, even down to the smallest of them."

H. H. Dilgo Khyentse Rinpoche says: "The blessings of all the buddhas pervade all those who have strong confidence and devotion. The sun's rays fall everywhere, but only through a magnifying glass can they set dry grass on fire. In the same way, only through the magnifying glass of your faith and devotion can the Buddha's compassionate rays focus and blaze up blessings in your being."

To make the fire of blessings burn more fiercely in our being and to incinerate the roots of the five poisons, please add on more firewood of devotion.

August 16

Carcass Remains

THE SHORT summer season went by swiftly; there are already telltale signs of autumn in the open fields. Even with some late summer flowers still obstinately standing tall, the sense of desolation associated with fall is unmistakably in the air.

About ten kilometers from Serthar and nearby Yalong Monastery is a place famous for its lush summer flowers. Hoping to catch the last glorious summer showcase there, Sodon, a few others, and I took off in high spirits. Sure enough, here and there the flowers, perhaps touched by our sincerity, stood with chins held high on the doomed green field and managed to convey a sense of flourishing liveliness. Likewise, the little brook, seemingly oblivious of the imminent winter freeze, hummed a polka-like tune as it rushed on. The babbling stream, together with the distant singing of shepherd boys and the neighing of horses, delivered a lively, welcoming chorus upon our arrival.

My companions settled down to start a fire for tea. Feeling awkward as a bystander, I strolled along the stream. Not too far away was a well-known charnel ground, supposedly on a par with India's Cool Grove, to which vultures fly over thousands of miles to feed. Khenpo Chang-chup Dorje's mother was sky-buried in this charnel ground after she died. I imagine that this site is a sacred place for dakinis to congregate. A rotten yak carcass caught my eye, and I wondered when and why it landed here. Its suffocating stench attracted many cesspit-chasing creatures, now swarming all over the skeleton. It looked disgusting and reminded me that my own sack of flesh and bones will soon decay.

Even though I know perfectly well that one day I will inevitably meet the same fate as this yak, I still toil all day long to serve this conjunction of body and mind. The yak's corpse was a life lesson, waking me up from oblivion, and I saw that all things in the world—the autumn of fading flowers, the ever-rushing brook, and the once strong-bodied yak—are teachers of impermanence. Arrested by a strong sense of renunciation, I prayed for the blessings of buddhas and dakinis that all beings lying in this charnel ground soon find liberation.

Time slipped away, and my companions called me from a distance. The sun soon sank halfway below the horizon. With a heavy heart, I walk back reluctantly.

August 17

Taste It

ISSUING bad verbal checks has never appealed to me. Merely talking about the Dharma, no matter how profoundly, without melding it into one's daily activities can only plant some good seeds in the mind but can do nothing to help in this and future lives. The *Avatamsaka Sutra* says:

> A Buddhist who does not put the Dharma into practice is like
>   a deaf musician playing music to entertain others but not
>   himself.
> A Buddhist who does not put the Dharma into practice is
>   like a boatman who ferries people across the waters but is
>   drowned himself.
> Sweet taste is experienced by mastication rather than descrip-
>   tions; likewise, emptiness is realized by practice rather than
>   words.

Therefore, the doctrines are not to be extolled only at the level of words, and their greatness can only be appreciated by actual practice and personal experience.

Some Buddhists have read the scriptures and the teachings of lineage masters extensively, but their knowledge remains within the pages of books. They are proud of their encyclopedic memory of the Dharma, yet they readily succumb to afflictive emotions. Technically, they differ not from a starved person describing sumptuous meals or a pauper counting others' money. The Dharma, the very sacred way to liberation, is reduced in their hands to tools to satisfy their vanity.

A Tibetan proverb goes: "Merely knowing the Dharma is not enough; we must practice it. Merely possessing food is useless; we must eat it." Therefore, we should let go of worldly trifles to enact the Dharma we have learned so that we can savor the exquisite taste of the Dharma day and night. Now that we have the key to the treasure chamber of liberation, we should try our best to gain access to it.

August 18

Monastic Ordination

A FEMALE college graduate from Dandong city came to me and asked to be ordained as a nun. Tall and slender, with pretty and delicate features, she is in the prime of her youthful years. Her decision, no doubt, must seem incomprehensible to many worldly people. Why not take this opportunity to find out what is in her mind? Her answer will also help to gauge the strength of her determination.

I asked: "Why do you want to become a nun? Many people think that for a young lady like yourself to enter a monastic life is akin to trampling on a pretty flower yet to bloom—it is inhuman. What do you think?" Hearing my question, she lost all of her shyness and fluently poured out her heart:

> To many, worldly living can satisfy a human's thirst for physical and mental comfort—owning cars, fine houses, and enjoying the much-glorified love relationship. To these ends, they invest all their effort, yet what they get in return is usually at odds with their wishes. Strive as they may, they can never feel content because desire only strengthens daily. People may boast extreme wealth or large retinues, but how many can find absolute freedom in a world where everyone tries to cheat or outwit others?
>
> As for the so-called love relationship, how many couples have made it until the end? Most love unions go up in smoke;

a breakup without bitterness is considered lucky. Now, would you deem such worldly living to be happiness?

To live a monastic life is not inhuman; on the contrary, it provides a way to find the true self through spiritual training. There is no greater happiness than to live a monastic life!

I was relieved after hearing her point of view. Clearly, her decision to become a nun emerged from serious and careful deliberation rather than on impulse. The *Great Treatise on the Perfection of Wisdom* says:

> Well-adorned with splendid feathers is a peacock, yet it is no
>   better than a goose that can fly long distances.
> Wealth and power a lay person may possess, yet such blessings
>   pale compared to those of the ordained.

Let's hope that we will have the expansive wings of the goose flying up into the vast sky of an open mind. Let's not crave the dazzling plumage of the peacock, as it weighs us down and prevents us from flying freely in the dharmadhatu.

August 19

Buzz Buzz

A TIBETAN RIDDLE about bees: "It is not a tiger, but it has a tiger's fur patterns; it is not a yak, but it sounds like a yak; it is not a rat, but it can fit in a rat hole." Bees, in any case, are always portrayed as being diligent and hardworking.

While having tsampa this morning, a big bee appeared and hovered around me, buzzing. According to Tibetan belief, a bee that circles a person is a relative yet to gain liberation in the bardo state who, granted leave by the Lord of the Bardo, comes searching for Dharma in a bee's body. To bless these restless spirits, Tibetans recite the mantra of Avalokiteshvara or Vajrasattva.

"Dear little bee, which relative of mine are you?" But my question was met with only a series of buzzing notes. Though the living and the dead were right next to each other, there was no language to communicate with, only this humming sound. How sad! I could say no more but tried my best to recite mantras and buddhas' names to benefit this relative of mine.

There are other stories about bees in the sutras. The *Karandavyuha Sutra* records this episode: When the compassionate bodhisattva Avalokiteshvara went to Sri Lanka, he saw thousands of creatures living in piles of excrement at a corner of Yekoumoujie city. Avalokiteshvara then appeared as a bee and buzzed to pay homage to the buddhas. Hearing it, all the creatures there made the same sound to honor the buddhas. Henceforth, they destroyed twenty kinds of self-grasping with the wisdom diamond, became bodhisattvas named Fragrant Lip, and took rebirth in the Pure Land of Great Bliss.

"Dear bee, maybe you are the emanation of a buddha or a bodhisattva. Please tell me, what's the hidden meaning in your buzzing?" But again, the reply was only the humming buzz. Whatever my visitor's true identity—a bardo being seeking help, an ordinary creature, or the emanation of an enlightened one—I think I can offer no better reception than to pray to the Three Jewels.

When we are in the garden enjoying delightful flowers or feasting our eyes on the immense green fields, we will also see many tiny bugs or cute creatures. At this time of leisure and delight, always remember the suffering of sentient beings in samsara and the kindness of our protector, the Three Jewels.

August 20

Beholding the Guru

WHEN WE BEHOLD our teachers with delight or feel tremendous joy upon hearing their names, we create great merit. Constant remembrance of our teachers naturally enhances our confidence in the Buddhist path. Having visions of the guru, the Buddha, or bodhisattvas in dreams or meditation are signs that the disciple has established an unshakable faith in the Dharma. Similarly, only a person with uncontrived devotion will see that nothing other than the Dharma can truly benefit oneself and others.

An authentic teacher is a bodhisattva who has generated, at a minimum, a relative bodhichitta of pure intention and application. To look at such a bodhisattva, whether with faith or covetousness, creates immense merit all the same. The *Sutra of One Hundred Karma Stories* relates this story: "A young Brahmin aroused great joy when he looked at the Buddha. Due to this merit, he was spared a rebirth in the lower realms for thirteen kalpas and was reborn in the god realms for thirteen kalpas, enjoying well-being and happiness. Eventually, he was born as a human and became a monk; through training in the *Thirty-Seven Elements of Enlightenment*, he attained the level of a pratyekabuddha."

Therefore arousing even attachment toward spiritual teachers, the embodiment of Three Jewels, results in considerable merit. In that case, what need is there to relate the merit for beholding or making offerings to them with pure and deep devotion? Spiritual teachers lead us onto the path free from all suffering. They are the boat that takes us toward the shore of liberation and is the source of all happiness. Whether happy or sad, we shall behold or remember our teachers with joy, unceasingly filling us with the nectar of blessing.

August 21

Sky Burial

ANCIENT INDIA was noted for its eight sky-burial sites. The Tibetan highland has many such places, large and small, and one is located at West Larung Mountain. The relatives of deceased Buddhists often bring their corpses here, coming in cars, horses, or yaks from hundreds of miles around, even as far away as Lhasa or Chamdo, which reflects people's deep faith in our precious guru, H. H. Jigme Phuntsok Rinpoche.

Each day, five, six, or up to a dozen corpses arrive at Larung. They are first ritually blessed in front of the Great Shrine Room and later sent to the sky-burial site.

To refresh my mind on the lesson of impermanence, I went to the sky-burial ground with others this afternoon, even though I wasn't feeling well. It's been a while since my last visit. What grand and striking scenery to behold! Prayer flags fluttered in the stark mountain wind; clear streams ran through the verdant grasslands; a flock of wild geese flew in formation, adorning the vast sky. Such idyllic scenery, however, could not cover up the rotten smell wafting up now and then from the other end.

Corpses were loosely lined up. Some were older people who died from illness, while others had perished in their prime; there were men, women, and even babies. They had worn clothing and ornaments of the rich or the poor, but now they were all in their birthday suits equally. The sky-burial master began his operation, and with the cooperation of vultures, the bodies of those who had been animate a few days ago were soon devoured with little remaining.

All living beings have an incredible drive for survival. Yet everyone, whether rich or poor, noble or humble, old or young, is powerless to interrupt the working of impermanence. Some people fear corpses and dare not go to the charnel ground. However, Jetsun Milarepa says: "The scariest body is the living body." Just take a look at societies governed by jungle law nowadays. Don't you think that is scarier than what is here at the charnel ground?

The bereaved wiped their tears silently, but they had no way to call back the souls of the departed. The vultures spread their wings and soon vanished from sight. I was left with a profound sadness that for a long while refused to go away.

August 22

Rich or Poor

A LAYPERSON SAID to me ruefully: "You have always instructed us to give up the craving for money. But during my practice, I often felt the necessity of having money. For instance, with money, we can make offerings to the sangha, release captured creatures, print Dharma books, fund disaster relief, and so on. We should not flatly deny the usefulness of money or feel uneasy owning it. In my opinion, we need to have money."

His words gave me plenty of food for thought. In the secular world, honest poverty is respected, but poverty itself is far from being extolled. The Kadampa's maxim "Base your mind on the Dharma, base your Dharma on a humble life, base your humble life on the thought of death, and base your death on a lonely cave" is unacceptable to ordinary people. I am not here to negate the usefulness of money, yet its benefit is minimal. For instance, money can't buy the satisfaction derived from meditation, creativity, or appreciating something. What's more, money will never bring practitioners the utmost liberation.

Milarepa was notorious for being a poor wretch; thieves invading his cave found nothing to loot, not even a single needle or a piece of thread. Our beloved Guru Jigme Phuntsok Rinpoche was penniless while studying in Shiqu and lived on a paltry daily portion of yogurt. The Sixth Patriarch Huineng, when staying with the Fifth Patriarch, was a penniless monk responsible for husking rice. Yet the brilliance of their realization surpasses that of a diamond, and the merit they accumulated is beyond the wildest dreams of the wealthy. With achievements transcending money matters, they smashed the blind worship of earthly wealth and power.

There is an adage:

> In poverty, commit yourself to cultivating personal integrity.
> In prosperity, devote yourself to the welfare of the world.

For a spiritual practitioner, generating uncontrived bodhichitta will help sentient beings and oneself. In addition, making mental offerings with pure intention is far more worthy than making huge material offerings with a tainted mind. The best offering to one's guru is to engage in meditation rather than offering money or goods.

There is an old poem:

> I dreamed of having tons of gold and thoroughly enjoying a
>   life of unlimited glory and abundance.
> Suddenly my pillow fell, and I woke up to meet with nothing
>   but bare walls and the blowing wind.

Do not be fooled by superficial monetary rewards; fame, glory, wealth, and prestige are fanciful dreams. Is it worthwhile to waste our human life, which is beyond redemption once lost, on amassing wealth through trickery?

August 24

On Bullfighting

A VISITOR GAVE me a photo album today. Although I know nothing about photography, I flipped through the pages to acknowledge his good intention. All of a sudden, a frightful scene seized my attention. A bull and a man dressed in white are engaged in a fight to the death. The bull's body is soaked in blood, splattering the man's clothes and staining them red. Unnerving and frightful glares shoot out from both their eyes. The title of this picture is "A Contest of Strength and Beauty," and it is beyond me why it was chosen. To me, there is not a single shred of strength or beauty in the picture. Instead, words for brutality, horror, and barbarism rushed into my mind.

Bullfighting is believed to have originated with the ancient Minoans on Crete. Today the spectacle is highly celebrated in Spain. Many artists and men of letters are inspired to hype it in various ways. For instance, there is the famous bullfighting-themed aria *Votre Toast (Toreador Song)* in Georges Bizet's opera *Carmen*, based on Prosper Mérimée's novella *Carmen*. Spain's tauromania and the bullring were celebrated by the American writer Ernest Hemingway in *The Sun Also Rises* and *Death in the Afternoon* as the only place where one could see violent death now that the wars were over.

For a long time, *bullfighter (matador)* was synonymous with *hero*. Many women consider it an honor to receive some piece of the dead bull from the winning "warrior" as a love offering. Fans see the skilled sword thrust that kills the animal as a refined performance. Alas, people have not outgrown the barbaric instinct that allows this atrocious spectacle to go on and even savor it. Thinking of this pains my heart, as if a sharp needle is pricking it. These poor bulls serve as entertainment and will surely die once sent to the ring, with no chance of escaping their predetermined fate. Once a bull rebelled, killing the bullfighter El Yiyo by puncturing his heart with its horns. In the end, the bull's stuffed head was displayed in a museum as a trophy declaring the final "victory" of humankind.

Reportedly, an Italian priest attempted to end the merciless killings. Taking extreme measures and disregarding his own safety, he jumped into the ring and tried to persuade people to stop the sadistic sport. The crowd, which had lost all reason, stoned him to death; his warm scarlet blood glittered on the chilly, hard ground of the ring. The priest's death made people pensive, and bullfighting was put on hold for some time. Although I cannot recall this priest's name, his bravery in the arena will remain engraved in my memory and in that of anyone with a clear conscience.

I don't mean to belittle the Spanish, nor are they the only ones to endorse bullfighting. But I am willing to risk the world's disapproval to point out the imprudence and absurdity of bullfighting. To sacrifice another's life for pleasure, excitement, to fill the blank mind, or to win the title of hero and the favor of women is perverted. The law of causality will deliver the final verdict of the winner and the loser. People who kill or rejoice in it cannot avoid meeting the Yama's unforgiving verdict. Should there be an opportunity, I will also follow the steps of that noble priest!

August 25

Visual Perception

FOR AGES, people admired the spectacular beauty of the sun rising and setting and believed that it did so from the Earth's horizon. Such a perception still prevails in some regions of the world, even though the heliocentric astronomical model has virtually supplanted the older view. In elementary school, we are taught that the sun does not move; rather, Earth's axial rotation causes the sun to appear as though it rises and sets in our sky.

Yet people still lean toward what they see with their eyes. If you told them that not only are our sense perceptions of sunrises and sunsets erroneous, but everything we see—the sun, moon, stars, mountains, and rivers—is also illusory, your audience would probably widen their eyes and wonder if they should check you into a mental hospital.

From antiquity, humans have fixated on what they see with their eyes. Believing that all visual objects truly exist, they become attached, feel aversion, or are indifferent to these objects and establish a view of the universe as inherently existing. People would flatly reject Buddhist cosmology and the descriptions of Buddha's Pure Land, since their direct sensory perception cannot validly prove such accounts. This kind of self-righteous attitude is shallow and confining. The *King of Samadhi Sutra* says:

> The eyes, the ears, and the nose are unreliable;
> the tongue, the body, and the mind are unreliable.

If the senses could be relied on,

what need would there be for the path of the noble ones?

This teaching explains that our six consciousnesses are not ultimate. For instance, the lively and pretty lady in front of you, if subjected to careful analysis, can be mentally dissected into skin, flesh, bones, blood, and other components, and even divided further into subtle, indivisible particles, which in the end are not intrinsically existent and are thus empty in nature. Such a bold conclusion will shock many ordinary people, yet it is a truism applicable everywhere.

Cows are partially colorblind and suffer from poor depth perception. To a goose, things look smaller than their actual size, which explains the goose's overbearing manner. For insects with compound eyes, an object looks very different from what we see. When sentient beings of the six realms, buddhas, and bodhisattvas observe the same world, their conclusions are poles apart. So how can the statement "to see is to believe" be ultimate and irrefutable? Never trust your own eyes!

August 26

Tibetan Antelope

I HEARD THIS news on the radio. A shahtoosh shawl made from the downy hair of endangered Tibetan chiru antelopes is worth $100,000 or even five times more on the Italian fashion market. This news will surely quicken the heartbeats of bloodthirsty merchants, and I worry that the lure of high profits will encourage people to brazenly defy regulations and sell and buy illicit goods. No matter how the law forbids hunting, Tibetan antelopes, I fear, will eventually meet their doom.

Across northern Tibet's vast and peaceful prairies, these antelopes have been living their full life spans harmoniously with human beings for generations. When this disaster suddenly befalls them, they are at a complete loss. How can these gentle antelopes fight against humans with weapons?

Now, imagine this scene: A wounded Tibetan antelope lying in the field sadly looks at the prairie with blurred vision and, with its remaining breaths, bids its final farewell to the setting sun. Surrounding their prey are poachers who congratulate themselves and laugh uproariously, relishing the thought of big money on the way. With immense pain and terror, the antelopes perish and wander into the bardo realm, the killers' rowdy voices still ringing in their ears.

Behind this fashion trend lies huge piles of Tibetan antelope skulls, and around every shahtoosh shawl lingers the antelope's unsettled soul. How can those who sell or buy the shawls not know this? How can they not tremble and be terrified when wearing such a shawl? Can they ever maintain an easy conscience?

Sonam Dargye, an animal rights advocate for Tibetan antelopes, was murdered. Yet little do the murderers know that in accomplishing what they consider a triumphant feat, they have also killed their conscience, destroyed their present and future lives, and severed the life cord for liberation and wisdom.

The plight of Tibetan antelopes is only a tiny chapter in the history of human cruelty. Still, if this savage behavior is allowed to continue or becomes more prevalent, the destruction of Mother Earth will happen in the blink of an eye. How many people care that Tibetan antelopes and other endangered animals face extinction very soon?

Sentient beings are perpetually cycling in the six realms, changing from one form to another. "The mills of heaven grind slowly but surely." Who can say with certainty that an animal birth is not their next destination? Who can ever sidestep the consequences of positive and negative actions? When humans stop at nothing to satisfy the demands of a sumptuous lifestyle, there is no escape from paying a tremendous price.

There is some encouraging news. People are becoming sensitive to the issue of animal rights and animal protection. I look forward to seeing the northern Tibetan prairie populated again with its native antelope, and I hope this earnest wish is not just a fool's dream of paradise.

August 27

Sweet Hometown

PEOPLE TEND to have sentimental attachments to their home-towns. A person drifting abroad for many years would like to return to his native land; those who have succeeded look forward to a glorious homecoming. Even Mr. Average, with nothing to show, or los-ers who feel ashamed of facing folks back home, still declare an infatu-ation for their homeland, saying, "Gentle breezes, please send my deep love back home." This nostalgic feeling toward one's native place will always be there, no matter how far one has traveled from it.

For me, the mere thought of the Zong Ta prairie that gave me life and nourishment is enough to cause my heart to ripple. Its running streams and verdant mountains—"blue as the water in ever-flowing rivers, blue as the distant hills shrouded in the mist"—never fail to kindle a subtle and indescribable reverie in me. However, this senti-ment is precisely the one to abandon for people on the spiritual path. Longchenpa once reminded future generations: "The hometown is the holding prison; you must sever attachments to it." Clinging to one's hometown propels perpetual cycling in samsara and brings about all sufferings. As the adage says: "To live is to recognize your true face; do not mistake a wrong place for your hometown." This life's hometown is only a temporary lodging for the body, a stopover on the long journey in samsara. A man with foresight and sagacity will not let the landscape of his hometown block his vision in search of the ultimate liberation.

"The moon is the brightest in one's hometown," says a poem. But to a practitioner, this hometown refers not to a geographic location on the map but rather the absolute hearth and home—our mind's true destiny, our mind as it is. We have found our way back to our ultimate hometown; when will we get there?

August 28

Real Burglar

A DISTRAUGHT NUN REPORTS to me that her place has been burglarized. Seeing her gloomy face, I try to figure out a way to solve her immediate living problems and, at the same time, comfort her with lighter topics. I tell her that possessing one thing is inviting one problem. Living in a bare house or owning nothing is not necessarily bad, and I say this from my personal experience.

Someone from abroad once gave me a length of exquisite fabric. After that, whenever I saw this beautifully wrapped gift on the table, I would waste my time thinking about how best to use it. This went on for a long time until one day it fell into the hands of a thief. Oddly enough, I felt relieved when I saw the bare table.

Not too long ago, my place was jammed with all kinds of stuff, and the clutter made it difficult to search for information or find items. Then I gave away the books and daily "necessities" unneeded for the time being. After that, my room became clean and tidy, and I could let out a deep sigh of relief.

For now, on his own initiative, the burglar assumes the responsibility of tidying up our house. We ought to feel grateful. However, we must meticulously guard against another crafty burglar so that we are not vulnerable—this dangerous one is none other than the great thief of our defiled emotions. Ordinary thieves seize only petty items and bring temporary inconveniences to our daily lives. But the thief of afflictive emotions has set greedy eyes on our ultimate bliss of liberation. It will steal the wisdom sword from us, blindfold us, and throw us into the pit of samsara. Its evils are too numerous to count.

Usually we are so upset with burglars who have stolen our possessions that we gnash our teeth, yet we neglect to see the thief of destructive emotions right under our noses. Which one of them causes more severe damage? If we get the answer right, we will watch for the real thief with eyes wide open.

August 29

Guest Spider

U PON AWAKENING, I recalled Mipham Rinpoche's teaching *In Praise of Light Offering to Manjushri*: to offer light to Bodhisattva Manjushri's image is meritorious. I immediately lit the extinguished butter lamps. While preparing to read the *Journal of a Dream Trip to Ming Shan*, I suddenly saw a big-bellied spider trying hard to crawl up the wall.

There are two kinds of spiders that I know of. The one commonly seen in summertime is the cunning "summer spider" that builds its web around the corner and waits patiently for its prey to get caught. The other is the non-carnivorous "autumn spider" that feeds on soil and feces and is not as manipulative as its summer cousin. My visitor was of the second type. I decided to poke a little fun at this tiny fellow: "Hey you, old spider! You seem so busy, but what for? It's about time you think of impermanence. Autumn is closing in and frost is out there on the ground. Although it is warm inside the house, your days are numbered. The Lord of Death will soon fetch you. Why are you so unworried?"

Hearing me, the old spider stopped, raised its head high, and sneered at me: "There you are, the pretentious practitioner. You always talk so nicely! Why don't you take a good look at yourself? You are graying at the temples, and your teeth are coming loose. How many seasons have you watched the geese flying south? How often has the warm spring water turned icy cold to your touch? Yet you have not practiced seriously at all. Now, shall I say you are excelling in your practice on impermanence?"

Feeling touchy, I retorted: "You are talking rubbish! Look at your potbelly; what did you have to loot to fill it to the brim? Buddy, you miss nothing when it comes to greed, hatred, and ignorance. What are you being so snobbish about?"

"Fine, I do have a big belly. But there is only dirt and feces in it, unlike you guys who hoard people's offerings or money dedicated to the dead. You don't even bother to make proper prayers. Don't you think your appetite is the bottomless pit?"

This spiky argument left me speechless and ashamed, and I could only relieve my embarrassment with a chuckle. Though it might be only a tiny creature, it was by no means dimwitted and was perhaps more clear-minded than some self-proclaimed wise guys. Utterly deflated, I tried to end my predicament and said pretentiously: "Since you are born a tiny creature, I don't know how to help you. Why not let me recite the Buddhas' names for you? Just hearing them brings tremendous merit, so listen carefully. The *Nirvana Sutra* says: 'There are four direct causes to attain nirvana: one, keep company with virtuous friends; two, listen carefully to the Dharma; three, recall and contemplate the teachings; four, put them into practice.'"

Hearing my words, the spider no longer acted naughty. Instead, it emitted a long faint wail and positioned itself tightly against the wall as if getting ready to listen with all its might and express gratitude. I then recited the names of Ushnisha Buddha, Shakyamuni Buddha, and other buddhas and bodhisattvas. After resting, the spider seemed delighted and crawled slowly up the wall.

August 30

Imbibing the Essence

THERE ARE too many things we need to learn in our short lifetime, the breadth of which is formidable. There are the Buddhist sutras and shastras, worldly sciences, technology, computers, foreign languages, and numerous other areas of study. Even with the best effort—studying around the clock, reading on every subject, and memorizing countless books—all we can hold on to is a droplet of water from the vast ocean of information.

In Buddhist study, becoming well-versed in the five major treatises alone will take a few decades. Hence, it is crucial to study with qualified teachers to grasp the essential points incisively. Jowo Atisha teaches in *Poems of Instructions*: "Life is short, knowledge is boundless, and there is no way to study everything we want to learn in our lifetime. The swan finds nectar in water and imbibes it; similarly, we should find the vital essence among the multitude of teachings and follow it scrupulously."

In Tibetan Buddhism, the Gelugpas take *In Praise of Dependent Arising* by Tsongkhapa as their focal study, the Kadampas' leading practice is impermanence, while the Nyingmapas' is the realization of the Great Perfection. Every practitioner should find the training best suited to their ability and concentrate on it with tremendous effort.

The Omniscient Longchenpa once taught: "Knowledge is as infinite as the stars in the sky; there is no end to all the subjects one could study. Therefore, when we have this human existence, we must stick to the practice that will enable us to seize the fortress of the dharmakaya."

In the little time we have left, isn't it most crucial to concentrate on the Great Perfection, the blessed wisdom-mind lineage, and attain the essence of Tathagata Samantabhadra?

August 31

In Comparison

A LAZY PRACTITIONER, even after a lengthy stay in a reputable monastery, will attain only minimal accomplishment compared with his diligent peers. The *Hundred Waves of Elegant Sayings* explains:

> Merely collecting knowledge but failing to practice, one's
> mind receives no benefit from the Dharma.
> A rock submerged in water for a hundred years is still impene-
> trable and remains dry.

On the other hand, a hardworking practitioner will amass a vast amount of merit in a relatively short time.

Today a Han lama reported the result of his recent practice to me. In the past year, nine months, and twenty-three days, he has done 1,000,000 full-length prostrations, memorized many scriptures, and kept his vow of silence nearly the entire time. He has also recited a prayer to H. H. Jigme Phuntsok Rinpoche 1,000,000 times:

> From the holy site of Mount Wutai
> the blessings of Manjushri entered into your heart.
> At the feet of my Guru Jigme Phuntsok Rinpoche, I pray:
> May I attain your heart transmission and blessings!

When he took his vows over a year ago, I paid no particular attention to it. Numerous individuals make pledges in my presence, but after a while their vows and texts end up on high shelves gathering dust. Should they remember later, the time is past and the opportunity long gone. For this reason, I usually maintain my reservations about promises made. However, this lama has steadfastly followed up on his practices, which is rare and admirable. With this kind of resolve, what aspiration will not come true?

Some people become pompous after they have studied the Dharma for years or have received empowerments and transmissions. In truth, they have yet to complete a single round of the 500,000 preliminaries, let alone achieve such a large amount in a year. If one is reluctant to sacrifice one's free time for practices, there is no point talking about benefiting sentient beings or generating bodhichitta.

Time is fleeting; what have we done as we look back over the past year, nine months, and twenty-three days? Won't we feel embarrassed when comparing ourselves with this Han lama? From now on, let us make good use of each day and waste no more time.

September 1

Autumn Sentiment

SUMMER'S PRIME is past; a knife-like wind and biting frost damage frail flowers and rob the meadow of its vigor. Though fully aware of the changing season, my adoration of summer lingers on and drives me once more to Jin Ma's field near the county seat. I fancied that with my sincerity, heaven might be moved to lend me a magic lasso to bind summer's runaway feet.

With me were Chime Rigdzin and Ngorba, who shared my wishful thinking. The day was blessed with an extraordinarily blue sky like a flawless sapphire. No wonder the great sages of ancient India used the autumn sky to describe mind's clarity. The sky and the earth stretched on and on with no boundary between them as far as the eye could see. A perfect setting to recite this poignant line: "The autumn river shares a limpid hue with the vast sky."

A pile of rocks carved with the Mani mantra caught my attention and steered my mind back to my boyhood when I chiseled the mantra on stones daily. I noticed a piece with an extra deep engraving. Whoever did it must have put in a lot of effort. Did his hands get blistered as mine did? Were they badly chapped? Numb? Frozen?

With a tenacity that commanded admiration, some little flowers stood tall and covered the browning field. Brightly colored butterflies danced among them, soothing our hearts saddened by impermanence. The fish, oblivious to the changing surroundings, still idly swam about, arousing an urge to use my body heat to keep the chilling brooks warm and spare aquatic beings from suffering the bitter cold. Mother Nature reminds me that life is but a dewdrop on a lotus leaf, and good times will inevitably end. Facing this immense classroom of impermanence, I let out a long sigh:

> Flowers in a riot of color, showing off in midsummer,
> are destined to wither and vanish in the fall.
> Graceful are bees and butterflies dancing;
> can they withstand a few days' frosts and cutting wind?
> Squandering life away when in one's prime
> soon brings deep remorse over lost youth.
> All phenomena by nature are impermanent.
> Wait no more and treasure life's every minute!

September 2

Tender Care

I N CLASS today, our revered teacher mentioned that a devoted, diligent monk had recently fallen sick and had no money for medical treatment. Rinpoche asked us to help this monk and said that many difficulties surface in one's spiritual pursuits, which he had experienced during his school days in Shiqu. Offering support to someone in need is more meaningful than putting the icing on the cake when food is plentiful. Rinpoche said that when there were fewer people here, he had always tried his best to give material aid to the Sangha, but as Larung has grown tremendously in size, he is now unable to do as much as he would like to help everyone.

Hearing what the teacher said, this monk, blessed by the teacher, will undoubtedly receive support from many of us. When cared for and helped by the teacher during adversity, the gratitude welling up in the student's heart is profound and will long remain. I am no stranger to this kind of feeling.

In 1984, when I arrived here with few resources, my life was arduous, as my dubious family provided no financial aid. Rinpoche let me settle down temporarily by lending me a room near the lama's Dharma hall used to keep goats. Upon his return from Xinlong, Rinpoche also gave me fifty yuan, which to me was a colossal sum of money, as I was penniless then. I lived on it for a considerable period.

At the approach of Losar, the Tibetan New Year, people do their festival shopping and then get together to celebrate. As a newcomer in a strange land, I had only a tiny bag of tsampa and no place to go.

I tried hard to drive away my forlorn feelings with reading, but the monotonous words lost their power to penetrate my mind. Becoming despondent, I took a walk up the opposite hill. People happily moved around at the foot of the hill, and waves of merry laughter resounded, yet all this felt remote to me; my loneliness lingered on and followed me with every step.

Suddenly a familiar figure caught my eye. In the distance, I saw Ani Mundron, the younger sister of our teacher, holding a bowl and limping toward the room where I lodged. Then she emerged without the bowl. Curious, I quickened my steps to get back to my place. No sooner had I pushed open the gate to my room than a tray full of buns and fried dough cakes greeted me warmly.

My goodness, the big tray was filled to the brim! Tears rushed to my eyes. Now I could enjoy a sumptuous Losar meal! What came to me were not merely fried dough cakes and steamed buns; more important was our teacher's loving-kindness and tender care. I invited a lama named Rigdzin Nyingma to share these delicacies with me. Although the treats were gone in a few days, Rinpoche's kindness sustained me through that difficult and embarrassing period.

September 3

On Taciturnity

M ANY PEOPLE would like to master the art of conversation. They eagerly work on verbal communication skills, hoping to apply them someday to win people's approval and admiration. Yet little do they know that spoken words often lead to great disaster.

An ancient adage admonishes: "Out of the mouth comes evil. The lips gate the mouth. Tightening lips prevents evil." Spoken words are like the wind—they move without feet and soar without wings. Inappropriate comments are impossible to retract. No wonder the sages have all observed: "Be apprehensive when you have to talk; be wary when you have spoken, as if facing extreme danger." We'd better zip our lips to allow no slips that would make trouble.

Usually written words are preceded by thoughtful deliberation; words blurted out, on the other hand, are often followed by belated judgment regarding their pertinence. The saying "Thinking comes before writing, but wisdom dawns after speaking" is truly a keen observation by the ancient sages.

As spiritual practitioners, we should especially tame our minds and refrain from talking about others' qualities acerbically. We may speak gently and fittingly to lead people onto the spiritual path. On other occasions, we should keep our mouths shut. Taciturnity is not a fool's mark, but loquaciousness quickly betrays one's triteness. The *Vimalakirti Sutra* says: "Guard your thoughts as if protecting a city; tighten your mouth as if sealing a vase." Humans are born with two ears but only one mouth, meaning we'd better listen more and talk less.

We shall refrain from making irresponsible remarks when we don't know what to say. Silence is always the best word.

September 4

Daily Schedule

I AM A greedy person. The main objects of my greediness are books and Dharma teachings, and I spend most of my time on these.

At four every morning, I must get out of my cozy bed. After the regular ritual of offering and recitation, I prepare for my teachings on *The Great Chariot: A Treatise on Finding Comfort and Ease in the Nature of Mind* and *The Precious Treasury of Pith Instructions*. I also review the translation of our master's teaching on the *Sutra of the Wise and Foolish*. At five, after a quick wash-up, I eat a little tsampa soup to boost my almost depleted energy. I then drag my reluctant body out of my home and walk to the classroom.

I teach between 6 and 8 am, and then 8 to 8:30 is for receptions. Every day, long lines of people have endless woes and joys to relate, and each story tugs my sensitive heart up or down. Often, I cannot but let the reception run overtime to best satisfy everyone's needs. Then a half-hour medical treatment follows—my lousy back eats up my precious time. No sooner do I try to read a little than it's time for the simultaneous translation of the *Sutra of the Wise and Foolish*, which goes on until 11:30 am. Only then can I go back home to catch my breath.

After shoveling food into my mouth, I begin my daily translation and writing. Translation now covers *Jewel Garland from a Mountain Hermitage* by Tulku Zagar, *The Journey to the Pure Land of Padmasambhava*, and the tantric portion of *The Great Chariot: A Treatise on Finding Comfort and Ease in the Nature of Mind*. My writing includes *Dispelling the Wrong Views* and my diary, *Glimpses from a Spiritual Journey*, but I've been tardy about daily entries and usually make it up a day after it's due. Whenever I take a break in the yard for more than ten minutes, I feel remorseful for wasting too much time, and I often close my door and unplug the phone to discourage unnecessary drop-ins. After finishing my daily recitations, I can finally crawl into bed at 10:30 pm to drift into sweet, relaxing dreams.

My tight schedule allows me no time to savor the many delicacies offered to me. I want to give them to others, yet I cannot afford the time for that and have to watch helplessly as the food passes the expiration date and deteriorates. Some people may consider me too self-absorbed. But thinking that these Dharma books will continue to benefit beings after I depart, I can't stop the pace of translation and writing for any reason.

September 5

On Jealousy

JEALOUSY is a widespread and highly destructive mode of the mind. Women are jealous of another's beauty; men are bitter about another's power; children envy those having toys they covet; hungry ghosts crave the food in another's hand. Jealousy comes in all shapes and sizes. The sages quickly noticed: "The gun shoots at the bird standing above the others. Thunderstorms and wind strike taller trees in the woods. Running water levels mounds that have accumulated by the water banks. Others will deride a man rising above his peers." Such insightful sayings run through the ages.

In world literature, Othello, the eponymous hero in William Shakespeare's play, becomes suspicious that his wife has betrayed him. In a jealous rage, he kills his wife and his imagined rival and then commits suicide. The legendary Chinese military general Zhou Yu was boldly confident at the height of his success:

> Dressed in a silk hood, with a plume fan in hand,
> brave and bright, laughing and jesting with his bride so fair,
> he sees his enemy ships destroyed as he has charted.

Yet Zhou Yu became so envious of the accomplished strategist Zhuge Liang that he could not help lamenting: "Why does Liang have to be in the world along with Zhou?" He then died in painful dejection. These tragic deaths are bemoaned generation after generation, but how many can declare with certainty that they themselves contain no shadow of Othello or Zhou Yu?

Even spiritual practitioners are not immune to jealousy. We feel invisible worms nibbling at our hearts when others are surrounded by adoring disciples, earning the master's high opinion and favors, or recognized for keeping perfect precepts and having superior wisdom or realization. Moreover, in meanspirited people who cannot tolerate others' gifts and virtues, these afflictive emotions will morph into hatred and trigger unwarranted character assassination. Such attacks only destroy both parties, at the very least. The perpetrator will likely become a laughingstock after exhausting his schemes to harm others and failing miserably. It is essential to understand that in the battlefield of envy, there is no booty to seize, only ruin. That being the case, why are we still gripped by envy?

Jealousy is the most frightful devil; it devours our reasoning. Jealousy is an inferno; it burns up all the seedlings of wisdom. Jealousy is the scorching sun; it dries up the fountain of compassion. We'd better annihilate this wicked root of all trouble before it destroys us!

September 7

Tidy Up

EVERYONE shares the responsibility of protecting the environment in which we all live. On this issue, no one can stand aside, aloofly indifferent. Whether we view it as a national, family, or personal issue, hygiene and sanitation affects us all directly.

Some urbanites are overly fussy about personal hygiene and grooming, spending three to four hours daily pampering the body or applying makeup. It's such a shame to waste valuable time! Meanwhile, some practitioners go to the other extreme. Deeming tidying up a time-consuming chore, they leave the dishes and laundry undone, hair and face unkempt, and houses and shrine rooms messy and dust-covered. All along, they think they have achieved a high level of insight. In fact, they not only hamper their health, but they also raise eyebrows.

If you are a yogi practicing alone in an out-of-the-way place, you can follow whatever whims you may have. But you should exercise caution if you have not realized the single state of equality and purity or are still living and interacting with others in the mundane world. The Basic Vehicle precepts and Vajrayana Kriya Tantra practices all emphasize daily ablutions and good hygiene. Paying attention to tidiness is beneficial to our practice and health.

Larung Academy is a big family with thousands of members, and Larung Valley is a sacred place where sages throughout the ages have meditated. We should take special care to protect Larung's environment, making it the ideal place for everyone to study, reflect, meditate, and fully imbibe the nectar of the Dharma. Of course, among all the practices to maintain cleanliness, the most crucial is that of the heart. Even if our house is spotless and our bodies fresh and neatly dressed, we must constantly turn inward to check if we have dusted clear our inner selves. We must know that keeping our hearts pristine is the ultimate hygiene.

September 10

Deep Woods

THE FOLIAGE alluded to in the poem "Splendid are the maples woods at dusk; I stop the carriage to gaze my fill" always stirs a sense of adoration in me. And I am fond of the Russian landscape painter Ivan Shishkin's deeply hued, solemn, and melancholy depiction of the woods. The lush, turquoise-hued forests framed by the blue sky and the snow-capped peaks in the distance always delight me.

Mountain forests are praised by countless spiritual seekers. The fresh air, beautiful flowers, limpid streams, and brilliant moonlight are untainted by the strife and hustle of the secular world and provide us with an ideal place conducive to spiritual growth. When exhausted physically and mentally, worldly people often seek out the woods to purge their worries, affording some respite for their weary bodies and minds.

Buddha Shakyamuni's birth, enlightenment, and nirvana were all manifested under the trees, signifying that trees have auspicious and inconceivable connections to spiritual advancement. The *Avatamsaka Sutra* says: "Rare is the fruit tree of wisdom, wonderfully planted with deep roots; adorned with increasing qualities, bodhisattvas' deeds shelter beings of the three worlds." The *Sutra on Rules of Excellent Intention* also declares: "The Buddha told Maitreya, bodhisattvas and his disciples ought to adopt these four ways . . . and the third, to always enjoy sitting or sleeping in the woods."

When practicing in the woods, we should take a break after long stretches of meditation or reading. Shifting our eyes around and looking at the green trees will help refresh our eyes and relieve bodily fatigue. The forest allows us to sweep the mind clean and throw away mental trash, thus revealing our fine qualities as immaculate as the moonlight.

Being spiritual seekers, we are more than just lovers of the deep woods. We shall cultivate the forest of wisdom merit. May we soon become a free-spirited garuda, spreading our wings and soaring over this virtuous forest of wisdom!

September 11

Making Preparations

AN INTELLIGENT person must prepare for the future. If you want a house built, you must secure building permits, architects and contractors, building materials, etc. If you plan to travel abroad, you must have your passport and visa. Similarly, as Dharma practitioners, we must prepare for our death. Shakespeare said: "The adder hisses where the sweet birds sing." We are happily living our interesting lives now, but death will come at any moment. Those who have attained realization feel confident that they can deal with death. However, for the majority of us, this is not the case. What, then, should we do?

In *Teachings on the Pure Land*, Mipham Rinpoche left a precious teaching that is particularly relevant to all of us these days: "Constantly generating strong faith and aspiration in Buddha Amitabha and his land, a veteran pure-land practitioner will be reborn in the Pure Land of Great Bliss. Moreover, the same result can also be facilitated even on the deathbed, when the dying person is made to hear the name of Buddha Amitabha and invoke an intense yearning for rebirth. This is made possible by Buddha Amitabha's powerful vows and the much keener consciousness that becomes very responsive to commands when dying and in the bardo state. With the sheer blessing of Buddha Amitabha's vows, one will immediately be reborn in his Pure Land by calling his name. Therefore, it is crucial to become familiar with these pith instructions and apply them in life, at the moment of death, and in the bardo."

How fortunate for us lazy ones to hear this truest and mightiest instruction! If we can be clear-minded, calling to Buddha Amitabha even for an instant when dying, we will have a chance to catch the very lifeline leading to the Pure Land of Great Bliss. Do not let go of it, no matter what!

September 12

Feeling Ashamed

I RECEIVE PEOPLE for consultations at 8 am daily. For half an hour or so, I find it hard to hold my sensitive heart in check as it swings according to the joys and woes of the visitors.

An incident today made me feel quite ashamed. Among my visitors, there was a newly ordained intellectual type. She implored others in line to spare her a little private time with me. When they agreed and had retreated, she handed me an envelope and said: "As a newly ordained person, I am not familiar with the rules here and hope I am not committing any infractions. But I have a request that I wish you would grant me."

After I replied in the affirmative, she continued: "After reading your article 'The Merit of Releasing Captured Creatures' yesterday, I came to see that life is most precious to any being in this world. As Mahayana practitioners, we should cut back on our daily needs, such as food and clothing, for other beings' lives. I do not have much money except this 3,000 yuan meant to buy myself a place to live. But now I've decided to forgo my plan and offer this money for the release of live beings. In the meantime, if it's not too much trouble, please help me find a temporary shelter. Is it possible? A tiny place to protect me from the elements would suffice."

I said: "You must consider this carefully. I'm afraid I can't find a temporary house for you now. If you give away this money, won't you have financial difficulties in the coming days?" "For my room," she replied, "I'll explore other possibilities. As for my living expenses, the 50 yuan monthly stipend should amply cover my daily needs. No, I will not regret my decision. Please help me to fulfill my wish."

Sensing her firm determination, I accepted the heavy envelope containing the cash that would benefit many lives. However, my heart sank like a stone when I thought of the harsh winter months she'd endure without a warm coat and a place to live. Biting my lip, I emphatically wrote three words on the envelope, "Fund for lifesaving."

As I watched her retreating figure, a sense of shame welled up in me. I have been prattling in the classroom and in books that we must do our best to benefit sentient beings without self-interest. Yet have I forsaken my needs and accomplished anything that would help others? Haven't I been talking and behaving just like a parrot? I recalled an old saying:

> A person could be called a deaf person if hearing of good
> deeds arouses no admiration in him.
> A person could be called a blind person if seeing good deeds
> arouses no respect in him.
> A person could be called a dumb person if he speaks not what
> he knows is right.

I am a person complete with five sense faculties. How could I not feel admiration and respect for such a good deed? How could I remain silent and not feel embarrassed? I give teachings to others every day, yet I was taught a lesson by another person today.

September 13

Unforgiving Avenger

IN MY August diary entry "Devastating News," I mentioned the abrupt death of Sangye Rangpo. His younger brother, intending to avenge his brother's death, has neglected his family responsibilities and goes about armed with a fury ready to explode at any moment. He has been roaming about for more than a month looking for the murderer, unconcerned about the elements or his hunger. Frustrated day by day, he is losing his mind, and his rage rapidly flares with increasing intensity. Any remaining drop of patience has all but evaporated, and he is utterly dominated by his pent-up fury. Should he manage to spot his nemesis, he will spare no time tearing him to pieces.

To ease his embittered mind, I decided to talk to him. However, my confidence that I could persuade him took a dive when I saw his wrathful eyes glaring as he stood before me. Obliged by a sense of responsibility, I braced myself and said, "You know, a dead person cannot be revived. It's no use crying over spilled milk or a broken mirror. All worldly affairs are predestined by karma, and what happened between the murderer and your brother was the unfolding of their unfortunate connections. Should you kill the perpetrator, you'll only pile up more sinful deeds of your own without doing your brother any good. Please be gracious and open-minded, and put this family feud behind you."

Hearing my words, he answered with obstinance and firm resolve: "My elder brother is dearest to my heart. Even a million yuan is not worth a little finger of his, let alone his life! If I fail to avenge my brother's death, I'll never be able to hold my head up in my hometown. Even if I am reduced to poverty or ruined, I still must retaliate!" Apparently he has burned away all notions of past and future lives and karmic law. There is no hope of making him come to his senses now; only the pounding waves of time can wear away his enmity and restore his reason.

Over the prairie, a lonely wayfarer rambles through the day. When will he look up to see the clear blue sky over his head and let his mind become just as vast and spacious?

Some people may deem this avenger heroic or brave because he is willing to sacrifice everything for the sake of his beloved sibling. Yet, this is precisely the pitfall that traps worldly fools. Mundane relationships change in the twinkling of an eye. In this life, people commit misdeeds at any cost to please loved ones. But who can tell what roles we'll play with one another in future lives? There is an adage:

> He eats his father's flesh while beating his mother.
> He embraces an enemy that once killed him.
> The wife is gnawing on her husband's bones.
> Samsara's ongoing dramas are just absurd.

Indeed, in the eyes of sages, worldly people have been playing round upon round of ludicrous dramas!

September 15

Compassionate Education

THE ENVIRONMENT in which a child grows up can shape her future disposition. For instance, a person raised in a loving atmosphere from an early age will naturally have a caring heart. A person exposed to respecting the Three Jewels from childhood will have a heart full of faith and devotion. Children's minds are pliable and responsive to healthy, positive influences.

On September 9, 1999, Thupten Norbu Rinpoche established an elementary school in Guoluo, Qinghai. Since then, he has seen it struggle through many difficulties as it continually improves its educational program, expands its curriculum, and upgrades equipment and facilities. The school now boasts ninety-eight students and sixteen faculty members.

Every day at 6:30 in the morning, the children are awakened by the melodious music of "Taking Four Refuges" to start their day. Once out of bed, they line up neatly and with folded hands bow to the Three Jewels, take refuge, arouse aspiration, and circumambulate the shrine room three times. The washing up starts at 7 am. Next, they go to the main hall, find their seats, and chant in unison with palms together:

> The unsurpassable teacher is the precious Buddha,
> the unsurpassable protector is the precious Dharma,
> the unsurpassable guide is the precious Sangha.
> To the supreme sources of refuge, the Three Jewels, we make
> offerings.

May we and all beings in every lifetime
never be separated from the Three Jewels.
By unceasing offerings to the Three Jewels,
may all be showered with the blessings of the Three Jewels.
By this pure and excellent virtue,
may all beings accomplish the two accumulations of wisdom
    and merit.
By the perfection of the two accumulations,
may we all attain the pure and excellent two kayas.

Following breakfast, daily classes start at 8 am. The main courses include reading and writing in Chinese and Tibetan. After lunch and a noon break, the afternoon program resumes at 2 pm. Dinner is at 6 pm, study hour is at 7 pm, and bedtime is at 9 pm. The teachers oversee all the activities, and only after every student is settled do they retire to their rooms.

These students are orphans or children from low-income families, and their births might have been disadvantaged or unfortunate. Still, they are being cared for and educated in a way that rivals or even surpasses that of children born into more privileged circumstances.

Children reared in such an environment—full of love, respect, and devotion—are like seeds endowed with a vital life force. In the future, they will definitely plant and propagate more seedlings of love, respect, and trust worldwide.

September 17

Sincere Counsel

A MONK ASKED me to give him advice. Feeling self-conscious, I told him: "I am but an ordinary monk, still besieged by heavy karma and mental afflictions. I do not even possess the full qualities of a good Dharma student. How can I confer upon you any worthy teachings?" Yet he was not discouraged by my answer and pleaded insistently. I finally gave in and, at the risk of overrating myself, managed to tell him the following in all sincerity:

I pay homage to gurus and yidams!

If we wish to attain accomplishments, we should always pray to the Three Jewels. The yidams are the root of all accomplishments; therefore, meditate attentively on your chosen deity. Dharma protectors are the roots of activity that dispels obstacles; therefore, constantly make offerings to them. To practice successfully, we must follow spiritual friends for years and meditate on impermanence in solitude. We may keep our practice going when we are provided with food and clothing, under fair weather, or in a good mood. But our efforts usually snap when we need food and clothing, are in a foul mood, or the weather gets too hot or cold. Worse, we may even stop practicing altogether. Such is the biggest weakness of most practitioners.

To an adept, everything that happens is conducive to practice; to a poor practitioner, everything is an obstacle.

How things appear is determined by one's attitude. There are 84,000 ways to practice, and there is a way best suited for each seeker, whatever the need is.

We must rely on authentic spiritual masters and serve them wholeheartedly and respectfully; by pleasing them, we'll receive tantric pith instructions. When we practice seriously with unshakable faith, the blessings of mind-lineage masters will eventually enter us, and we will realize the nature of the mind.

The richness of the Great Perfection is incomparable to all the wealth in the world, and it is graspable only when we have conviction and personal experience. When abiding in Great Perfection, our mind remains calm like a waveless sea—even if there are violent storms outside, even if the world is scourged by war or plagues, even if beasts and floods attack, or even if millions of people forcefully manipulate us.

The monk took quick notes as he listened and left my place contentedly after hearing it all. Even though I might have said something worthless, nonetheless, it represented my heartfelt counsel. Here I am writing down the gist of it, hoping it may benefit some individuals.

September 19

Buddhist Doctrine

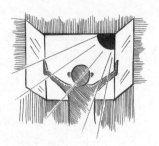

T HE WORLD has witnessed the emergence of rare or fantastic
things through the ages. In the current era, science and technology have ushered in new trends, epochal inventions, and ever-
changing concepts and ideas. Many traditions are subject to scrutiny
as never before. Some traditional faiths and religions face identity cri-
ses or fail to keep up with the pace of time, becoming stagnant. However, others have responded differently. When waves pound the shore
and wash away sand, genuine gold becomes more splendid—thus,
Buddhism shines even more brilliantly under the siege.

Curious Western scholars initially investigated Buddhism in a nit-
picky way. However, after conducting exhaustive theological, psycho-
logical, and scientific studies, they could not find fault with Buddhist
doctrine. Instead, Buddhism has proven to be an eye-opener, providing solutions to many of their long-standing puzzles. They discovered
remarkable outcomes when applying Buddhist concepts to clinical
therapy, hospice care, and other areas. Thus, they feel compelled to
assume a new stance in investigating this ancient wisdom.

Their research has concluded that Buddhism is not merely a religious
belief, as commonly believed. Rather, it is a study of the mind that sub-
sumes philosophy, science, medicine, literature, and many other disciplines. Indeed, Buddhism's wisdom is unfathomable to the ordinary
human mind. The Buddhist view soars high in the sky with tremendous
foresight and a commanding air. Like the fabled Shangri-La, it manifests itself majestically to Westerners, dazzling them. Astonished and

awed, they abandoned their earlier biased opinions to accept or even identify with Buddhist perspectives.

In the *Sutra of Dense Array*, the Buddha says:

> O monks, just as a goldsmith tests gold by rubbing, burning, and cutting before buying it, so too, you should examine my words before accepting them, and not just out of respect for me.

The classical process of discerning genuine gold from false minerals involves sixteen rounds of firing and rubbing, plus detailed examination and analysis. The Buddha urges us to apply an equally rigorous authentication method to his teachings and never mandates that one submit to power or authority with blind respect. In Buddhist training, phenomena are analyzed in three ways: by direct perception, by inference, and by scriptural authority, which accords with scientific methodology or even supersedes it in some aspects. The Buddhist maxim "from emptiness all phenomena arise interdependently" will, like pure gold, timelessly endure the blasting furnace's fire.

In this era of scientific advancement, wise people may embrace all possibilities with a broad vision rather than become complacent, confining themselves in the darkness of prejudice and belittling what is incomprehensible. Open the tightly closed windows widely; a lovely and bright spring scene will greet you!

September 20

Mid-Autumn Festival

TODAY is the Mid-Autumn Festival, when people naturally think of the moon. The moon this evening is said to be at its fullest, brightest, and most charming. When the full moon emerges high up in the ebony sky, the clouds all but vanishing, it is customary to have a family reunion to behold and enjoy its beauty. This tradition, plus the rich legends associated with the moon—Chang'e flying to the moon, Wu Gang cutting the laurel, Jade Hare making heavenly medicine— give this festival a romantic flair.

According to the *Book of Zhou Rites, Spring Section*, in the Zhou dynasty thousands of years ago, the custom of "welcoming winter," "offering warm garments," and "paying homage to the moon" was observed around the mid-autumn period. Eating mooncakes during the Mid-Autumn Festival reportedly began in the Yuan dynasty. At that time, Zhu Yuanzhang led Hans to resist the tyrannical Yuan dynasty, and he hid messages in mooncakes that people exchanged as festival presents. Chu eventually succeeded in founding the Ming dynasty.

To those on the Dharma path, no tyranny is greater than the afflictive emotions, and to drive them out is, in a way, our revolution against tyranny. In 1995, I offered the *Treatises on Thirty Pieces of Advice* as a gift to practitioners, which may have been better than mooncakes. This year I am offering you the newly translated *A Journey to the Pure Land of Guru Rinpoche*, an additional antidote to overcoming negative emotions.

The mooncake is round, symbolizing togetherness and the wish that beloved family members never part from one another. But we all know that anything labeled "forever" would be an oddity in our ever-changing cosmos. As a famous poem goes, "People have sorrow or joy, they part or meet; the moon is bright or dim, she waxes or wanes." How many families can be guaranteed to always stay together? While we look skyward, admiring the lovely moon, shouldn't we also lower our heads to contemplate deeply life's impermanence?

September 21

No Alternatives

AFTER our guru's teaching on the ruthless killer Angulimala (*Garland of Fingers*), I rushed to the county seat in town to ransom doomed animals. It seems that a few slaughterhouses have found their way here overnight, turning a town once filled with the sweet smell of tsampa and butter into a place permeated by a nauseating, bloody odor.

I purchased twenty yaks from one slaughterhouse, thirteen from another, and still more from other butchers; altogether, eighty yaks were rescued from the knife. These yaks looked miserable. From the day they were hauled away from their familiar feeding pastures to this place that almost became their execution ground, they have not eaten or drunk. It's not hard to imagine their unbearable hunger and thirst. We quickly fed them hay and nectar water, blessed them by touching the tops of their heads with sacred scriptures, and hung a red cord around their necks, signifying their liberation from slaughter in this life. They will be released in a meadow where they will live their remaining years without a care.

However, the karma of sentient beings is not something we can control. There was this black yak that the butcher refused to sell to us for liberation, however much we tried to persuade him. His excuse was a shortage of meat, but when we bought some meat for him and even raised the price ridiculously high, he still wouldn't budge. This incident became our gravest regret that day. Sadly, I looked at this yak as it gazed at me intently. Its big, open eyes spoke volumes about its frantic grief and indignation, making me feel utterly discouraged and ashamed. Unable to bear the yak's pleading reproach, I could only do my best to recite mantras and buddhas' names to assuage its deep sorrow.

On this day, the cruelty of killing in this town might have subsided somewhat, but these tragic scenes will continue to play out tomorrow. What kind of world is this?

October 4

Men vs. Women

DURING China's National Day, celebrated on October 1, many visitors from different regions of Han China arrive at Larung, and extra coordination and security measures are enforced to accommodate them.

A group of lively young men and women from Beijing have been scheduled to meet me for an hour. Some are translators from the State Department, others are reporters from media units, and the majority seem to have had some exposure to Buddhism. A well-known female reporter asks: "Many Buddhist scriptures describe the defects of women. Why does the Buddha favor men over women?" Facing this modern youth who stands for equality between the sexes, I reply calmly: "This is not a question that only Buddhists need to address, but rather an awkward situation presented to the world as a whole. The issue of women's non-dominant position is not unique to Buddhism. Look at the world—isn't it true that very few countries have a woman commander in chief? Looking back through thousands of years of human history, how many women stand out as forceful stars of their generation? Now, try to count on your fingers: Among the innumerable activists that have come to the fore, what percentage are women?" Hearing my words, the group chuckled, and the lady reporter also lowered her head in deep reflection.

"As for Buddhist practice, as long as a woman has aroused strong faith and cultivated wisdom and compassion, she is much superior to any man who knows not to act according to the principle of cause and effect. In Vajrayana, the woman is the symbol of wisdom, and there is no issue with the inequality of the sexes. Many great female Buddhist practitioners, such as Dakini Machig Labdron, Dakini Yeshe Tsogyal, and others, have arisen in Tibet. They have left incredible legacies for future generations. How could any ordinary male be on par with them? So, if one day you enter the Vajrayana path and become a genuine practitioner, you will deeply realize the equality of men and women at a higher level."

Hearing my reply, the visitors appear satisfied. Presently, the meeting coordinator announces: "Visiting time is up!" Reluctantly, they take their leave from the reception room.

October 5

Fall Foliage

SITTING ALONE by the window, I quietly watch the shadows of the trees shifting inch by inch. The chilly autumn wind rustles the leaves, and golden colors tinge the mountains.

At this time last year, I toured Jiuzhai Valley, renowned for its breathtaking fall scenery. Tourists from various places travel long distances to fully imbibe the autumn splendor that is beyond depiction, even by the magic brushes of impressionist artists. Here, our Serthar Valley also boasts stunning fall foliage; the scale is smaller, but the scenery is no less breathtaking. Serthar literally means "golden plain." Each tree stands out like a striking brushstroke in the fall landscape, perfectly complementing the red cabins, the golden mandala hall, and the glazed roof tiles. All of them delight our senses in a way unrivaled by artificial colors. What's more, while immersed in this natural beauty, one feels the holiness of a buddha realm, enabling it to outshine Jiuzhai Valley, which leans more toward the showy and flashy.

I picked up a leaf that had just fallen. This spindle-shaped orange leaf shone brightly in the sunlight, and the central vein still had the rich green of its younger days, even though the leaf's edge was parched brown and curled up. Am I not just like this leaf? My physical body is now voicing complaints as the aging process has commenced. Yet my mind, refusing to give in to old age, still holds the toughness of younger days. The leaves are destined to fall to the ground, and each person will meet their end. Such is the fate of all. Thus, I feel a sense of camaraderie with the voiceless leaf. However, this leaf has the edge

over me because after it falls to the ground, it will transform into nutri-
ents to nourish the soil. In contrast, as a human, I will be blown about
by karmic winds in the intermediate state and end up in another rebirth
despite wishing otherwise.

> This ruined hall, empty and dilapidated,
> has seen better days bedecked with luxuries.
> This wasted lot, strewn with dead weeds and withered trees,
> was once a court dazzling with songs and dances.

Everything in the world is transitory. No matter how prominent
and majestic we may be, in the end, we are no better than a mere leaf.
Thinking this, what is there to be pompous about?

October 6

Making Choices

KHENPO TSULTRIM LODRO ransomed more than seventy yaks in three truckloads in Chengdu. To find these yaks a good home, I traveled to Luoho yesterday, skipping today's afternoon teachings.

As I neared the meat-processing factory, the sound of the yaks' whining reached my ears. Rushing over, I learned that eighty newly purchased yaks had been earmarked for slaughter today and tomorrow. These yaks were lashed up tightly against one another, and the carcasses of their butchered brethren were littered nearby. As if sensing the same awful fate, the yaks stared at one another mutely, their eyes teary. How could I not feel heartbroken to witness such a devastating situation? Master Lian Chi's saying came to mind: "In the world, the most precious thing is life; under the sky, the gloomiest place is the slaughterhouse!" So far this year, they have slaughtered 221 yaks, a significant drop from the four thousand sheep and three thousand yaks killed in 1995. All these yaks are animate living beings capable of feeling pain and pleasure, just like humans.

Yesterday morning, several Dharma friends, learning that I was coming to save lives, sent donations that amounted to over 10,000 yuan. Yet this sum was far from enough to buy all the yaks. I spent the whole evening negotiating with the owners. At length, we settled on 1.6 yuan per *jin* of weight plus 0.9 yuan per *jin* collectively for travel expenses, cold-room electricity, and feed. After weighing the yaks today, a total price of 177,000 yuan emerged. Not having enough money forced me to bargain with them, coaxing and importuning with all manner of reasoning, for another three to four hours. Finally, we agreed to drop the purchase price to 150,000 yuan. Although this price was on the high side for this region, the value of life is beyond any measure of money.

During negotiations, I searched my memory for any funds that could be mobilized. Then I remembered a sum amounting to 100,000 yuan that Dharma friends offered me for printing the *Treasure of Sutras and Tantras* and the *Treasure of Supreme Dharma*. I know I have to bear the consequences of shifting the usage of donated funds. Yet the story of the Zen master Yongming Yanshou has always lingered in my mind, that he bravely faced execution for his crime of taking government funds to release live beings. The masters of the past have left us ideal examples; I had no reason to hesitate.

At 4 pm, these yaks, plus a few purchased at the roadside, altogether ninety or so, were specially marked. We recited mantras and blessed them on their way to ranches to live out their lives peacefully, leaving the bloody slaughterhouse behind. The crowds, witnessing this happy occasion, rejoiced and clapped their hands cheerfully.

Although physically exhausted, we were all happy with our decisions and, in a buoyant mood, returned to Larung around 5 pm. That night, I had a wonderful dream: a herd of yaks came to me, paying homage and thanking me. Waking up relaxed and buoyant, my whole body felt as fresh as a rose. Lama chen!

October 9

Be Cautious

IT SNOWED lightly all night, and the wind sent the snow flying in the morning. The little lama next door was going out to fetch water when the old lama cautioned him: "The ground is very slippery, be careful!" But the little lama blithely ignored the warning and shot out. No sooner had he gone out the door than he fell with a thump and screamed.

Kindhearted people always remind others of looming dangers: "Do exercise precaution!" That said, many people still suffer severe consequences for their carelessness. To students on the spiritual journey, teachers also give warnings: "Be scrupulous!" Students should cautiously guard the three doors of body, speech, and mind; maintain mindfulness in all activities of walking, sitting, standing, or sleeping; and eradicate evil. If students ignore the teacher's words and become distracted and slothful, they will lose mindfulness and vigilance and go astray. Sadly then, it is too late to turn back.

The scholar Xue Xuan of the Ming dynasty says: "Great accomplishment comes from painstaking cautiousness." And Master Hong Yi says:

> Noble and upright integrity is cultivated from strict self-
> discipline when no one knows it;
> epoch-turning prowess is tempered by the prudence and fear
> of facing a deep ravine and thin ice.

That is to say, integrity as bright as the vast sky is cultivated in a humble and dim cottage; the command powerful enough to bring about radical change comes from extreme caution, as if standing on a cliff's edge or walking on thin ice.

Emulating our forefathers, we should always keep a highly alert, vigilant mind. Only by doing so can we uphold dignity and decency, be alert and not slacken, and attain our ultimate goal.

October 14

Barren Field

I HAVE BEEN FULLY occupied today by all kinds of trivial matters and have had no time to make sense of my jumbled thoughts. No decent shoot has sprouted from the field of my mind.

October 20

Blank Mind

I AM NOT FEELING well; my mind is a complete blank. A passage in the *Platform Sutra of the Sixth Patriarch* came to mind:

> The mind's capacity is vast and great like space, and has no boundaries. It is not square or round, great or small. Neither is it blue, yellow, red, or white. It is not above or below, or long or short. It is without anger, without joy, without right, without wrong, without good, without evil, and it has no head or tail. All buddha lands are ultimately the same as space.

October 22

Desolate and Bleak

M Y MIND is still bleak. Today, disciples of the Fourfold Assembly are enjoying the bliss of Dharma under the protective umbrella of our precious guru. Should impermanence strike one of these days, won't we become like orphans wandering helplessly in a deserted plain?

Lama chen!

October 23

Dharma Assembly

THE PURE LAND Dharma Assembly (The Dewachen Puja) is one of the four annual Dharma assemblies held regularly at Larung Buddhist Academy. Last year, due to Rinpoche's illness and other issues, this Dharma assembly did not occur. This year, however, government authorities have issued permission and it will be held as usual—for eight days, from today until the 31st.

Hearing this exciting news, devotees from various regions, young and old, quickly spread the word and have been coming to Larung in droves. In two days more than ten chartered buses have arrived. Huge crowds throng the sunny slope of Laity Ling, and all hearts pound with immense joy. Our beloved Guru Jigme Phuntsok Rinpoche has not appeared due to his poor health. Venerable Jetsunma Muntso bestows the cherished Empowerment of Buddha Amitabha upon the participants, who receive it with deep faith and devotion.

The daily schedule of the Pure Land Dharma Assembly is as follows: 8 am, start the recitation of *The Aspiration of Samantabhadra*; noon, recite *The Practice for Swift Rebirth in Buddha Amitabha's Pure Land* by Terton Lerab Lingpa; afternoon, recite the *Aspiration Prayer to Be Born in the Land of Bliss* by Chagme Rinpoche and the Amitabha Buddha's heart mantra; 6 pm, end the day's practice.

Every participant is required to recite the Buddha Amitabha's heart mantra 300,000 times. Many scriptures state that if one accomplishes the necessary number of recitations and meets the four requisite conditions, one will be reborn to Buddha Amitabha's Pure Land of Great Bliss. The four conditions are:

1. visualize the pure land
2. accumulate merit and purify obscurations
3. generate bodhichitta
4. make pure aspirations and dedicate all sources of virtue so that oneself and others may be reborn in the Pure Land of Great Bliss

Our Dharma Assembly provides the outer circumstances to fulfill the four conditions, and each individual strives in their mind to meet the inner aspects.

Numerous examples have proven that by engaging in *The Practice of Swift Rebirth in Buddha Amitabha's Pure Land* and reciting the mantra earnestly, we will be reborn in the Pure Land through the sheer blessing of Buddha Amitabha.

The setting sun shines on Larung Valley; golden sunbeams light up maroon-and-yellow monastic robes—what a spectacular scene! Beholding it, we cannot help but feel invigorated and high-spirited. May all beings be reborn in the Pure Land of Great Bliss!

October 24

This Auspicious Day

TO EVERYONE who has a connection with me, whether or not you know me personally: I wish you a happy day on this auspicious day of Lord Buddha's Descending from Heaven, one of the four major festival days in the Buddhist tradition.

The origin of this celebration goes back to when the Buddha, to repay his mother's kindness, went to the Heaven of the Thirty-Three to expound the Dharma to her. After that, the Buddha returned to Earth, and this festival marks the day of his descent from heaven.

On this auspicious day, the merit of performing any virtuous act will multiply boundless times. Therefore Tibetans often choose to hold pujas during this period, such as the Pure Land Dharma Assembly we are having. Numerous devotees pray in unison to Buddha Amitabha for rebirth in the Pure Land of Great Bliss.

After this assembly, H. H. Jigme Phuntsok Rinpoche plans to transmit *The Words of My Perfect Teacher*. This book, composed by Patrul Rinpoche, teaches the fundamentals and contains the essential guidelines for all basic sutra and tantra practices, culminating in the Great Perfection. Imbued with supreme blessings from the mind lineage, it is the indispensable pith instruction on the unerring spiritual path.

Nowadays, many practitioners attach firmly to their schools and reject other lineages, thus multiplying their afflictive emotions and estrangement from the authentic Dharma. Such sectarianism signals one's lack of proper understanding of the Dharma essence.

Sincerely, I suggest that we all let go of narrow-mindedness, whether we are Tibetan Gelugpas, Nyingmapas, or devotees of the Han Huayan or Pure Land practice. If we can follow the stages of training in this book—beginning with recognizing the preciousness of human existence, the impermanence of life, the defects of samsara, and the transference of consciousness later on—and advance step by step, we will purify defilements, eradicate the three poisons of the mind, and grow in wisdom and bodhichitta. In short, we will undoubtedly reap unimaginably bountiful harvests.

Through the pure intent of our guru, the Wish-Fulfilling Jewel, to expound on this teaching, may we eliminate the current disputes between sects and develop the right view and understanding. Marching hand in hand, may we cross the rapids of life and death, reach the other shore, and enter the fort of liberation.

In today's cities, there are so many Buddhist books in which authentic and false doctrines mingle, making it difficult to discern which is which. Many practitioners, even having received multiple instructions or met scores of khenpos and tulkus, still lament that they have yet to meet the authentic Dharma and genuine spiritual teachers. To them, this book will unquestionably prove to be the priceless jewel of Dharma nectar.

Like a bright lamp, it radiates light on our thorny path of
    spiritual practice.
Like a ship, it carries us across the turbulent ocean of samsaric
    suffering.
Like the sun, it brings limitless warmth to our dark, cold Saha
    world.
Like a spiritual friend, it imparts to us immaculate instructions
    toward liberation.

I earnestly hope that faith will arise in everyone who encounters this book, and by practicing seriously per its instructions, may all attain rock-solid right understanding and ultimate enlightenment!

October 28

Becoming a Vegetarian

IT'S MIDNIGHT. Sitting alone with a cup of tea, I enjoy the silent beauty of the chilly night. My mind, tangled up in all sorts of activities these past few days, finally has a chance to calm down. By my side, the book *Letters on Great Compassion* by the renowned master Shapkar Tsogdrug Rangdrol quietly calls for my attention. Even though I am exhausted physically, I start reading it in the dim light. Soon my ruffled mind is soothed by its earnest advice, and I immerse myself again in the chapters that admonish killing and advocate vegetarianism.

Closing the book, I let my thoughts gallop freely: Animals have always been humans' closest companions on Earth. The sparkling lakes, the lush emerald pastures, and the deep forests are their sweet homes. Generation after generation, animals live in various niches provided by Mother Nature. They flourish and blend well with heaven and earth, presenting a serene and pleasant world picture. Yet humans often rob them of their peacefulness. The animals, possessing neither weapons nor exceptional strength, may wish to live harmoniously with humans. However, such a wish is thoroughly crushed, like a bubble, by the onslaught of ruthless human behavior.

The atrocities inflicted on animals by humans have played out shockingly. The young butchered in front of their mothers, their flesh and blood devoured. With so much crimson blood splattered and carcasses littered around, the animals' sweet homeland has become a scene of utter desolation. The beautiful landscape, enshrouded by fear and misery, will soon fall into darkness. At the same time, humans' irresponsible killing is a major cause of worldwide disasters such as famine, epidemics, and wars.

Contemplating this makes my heart tremble. Shaken, I ask myself: By eating meat, am I not a willing accomplice to those who kill living beings? I scold myself repeatedly, and the pit of my stomach tightens. I was brought up to eat meat and have become habituated to it. After entering Buddhism, I tried to abstain from meat several times, but those attempts were aborted for various reasons. Even though the wish to become a vegetarian has always been deep in my heart, it's not powerful enough to crack the strong fortress of my bad habit. However, through tonight's reading and my recent reviews of related teachings, I now feel a sense of repentance lashing my recalcitrant mind, and the fire of compassion finally blazes in my heart. A surge of motivation makes my long-dormant wish germinate so that I can no longer devour my parents' flesh callously and at will.

I decide to refrain from eating meat for a year, starting today. I will also write articles, using my deep reflections on vegetarianism and no-killing as a reminder to myself and others. May the breeze of love blow away hostilities in our hearts; may the warmth of compassion disband the age-old harsh action of taking others' lives.

In the *Parinirvana Sutra*, *Lankavatara Sutra*, and other Mahayana scriptures, as well as in the teachings of eminent beings like Masters Lien Zi and Ying Kuang, there are ample examples of the immense merit of saving lives and the grave fault of eating meat. Master Hong Yi has specifically pointed out:

> Animals are not different from us.
> They are also living beings, only with duller minds.
> We should instead be compassionate toward them.
> I ask all of us to stop killing and to save animals' lives.
> Refraining from eating their flesh is called loving all beings.

Love and compassion should be the eternal theme of humans. But many obstinate Buddhists, myself included, have remained untouched, despite the volumes of teachings on compassion. Meat eaters satisfy their palates at the cost of other beings' lives and suffering. What makes it worse is that some people with ulterior motives rashly sacrifice animals while proclaiming the practice of secret Mantrayana. To be genuine spiritual practitioners, we should ask ourselves: All animals have been our parents previously; if we remain numb when feasting on their bodies, do we claim this act is a sign of realizing the indivisibility of purity and equality?

The distant Milky Way reminds me of the coming and going of time and tides. Human civilization has made quantum leaps and has achieved new heights. How can we not outgrow the primitive habit of hunting and brutality? In the West today, vegetarianism is a refreshing, growing movement; I believe this trend will spread worldwide and reduce the number of animals killed. May the warm breeze of Dharma soon dispel the dark cloud of taking lives; may the sun of compassion rise in the hearts of all beings and shine brilliantly!

December 11
Midnight at Barkam

About the Author

KHENPO SODARGYE was born in Tibet in 1962 in what is today the Sichuan Province of China. After spending his early years herding yaks, he entered Larung Gar Buddhist Institute in Serthar, first becoming a monk in 1985 under the great Jigme Phuntsok Rinpoche and then going on to become the preeminent scholar of Larung Gar. Khenpo has taught and translated the Dharma for over thirty years and has lectured on Buddhism and social issues in over a hundred universities around the world. He has been especially effective in popularizing Tibetan Buddhism among Chinese communities and regularly speaks at universities in Asia and the West.

What to Read Next from Wisdom Publications

THE DIAMOND CUTTER SUTRA
A Commentary by Dzogchen Master Khenpo Sodargye
Khenpo Sodargye

Learn from a beloved modern master and the ancient wisdom of the *Diamond Cutter Sutra* how to cut the attachment to all phenomena, especially emptiness, and hold on to virtue.

WHAT MAKES YOU SO BUSY?
Finding Peace in the Modern World
Khenpo Sodargye

"*What Makes You So Busy?* is a wonderfully down-to-earth, practical volume of wise counsel. Khenpo Sodargye shows the way to find happiness and contentment whether one is a monastic leading a life of seclusion or a layperson immersed in a socially active way of life. In doing so, he has done us all a great service." —B. Alan Wallace, president, Santa Barbara Institute for Consciousness Studies

THE NYINGMA SCHOOL OF TIBETAN BUDDHISM
Its Fundamentals and History
Dudjom Rinpoche
Translated and edited by Matthew Kapstein and Gyurme Dorje

"A landmark in the history of English-language studies of Tibetan Buddhism."—*History of Religions*

TALES FOR TRANSFORMING ADVERSITY
A Buddhist Lama's Advice for Life's Ups and Downs
Khenpo Sodargye

Enjoy a variety of meditations on topics from flattery and jealousy to karma and compassion. Drawing on adages from the Buddha, Confucius, and even Mark Twain, Khenpo Sodargye delivers simple and timeless insights about facing adversity and developing a good heart.

ALWAYS REMEMBERING
Heartfelt Advice for Your Entire Life
His Holiness Jigme Phuntsok
Translated by Khenpo Sodargye

In memory of the thirteenth anniversary of the passing of His Holiness Jigme Phuntsok, this memorial book was compiled based on audio recordings of his precious and renowned teachings. It includes stories of the lives of great masters and the four great Dharma gatherings at Larung Gar, as well as teachings on the principle of cause and effect, keeping an open mind toward all religious traditions, spreading the Dharma and benefiting sentient beings, and mastering what to adopt and what to abandon.

APPROACHING THE GREAT PERFECTION
Simultaneous and Gradual Methods of Dzogchen Practice in the Longchen Nyingtig
Sam Van Schaik

"Van Schaik's lucid explanation of the issues and technical vocabulary in the 'seminal heart,' or *nyingtig*, teachings provide the reader with an essential framework for tackling the extensive primary source material found in this work." —*Buddhadharma*

About Wisdom Publications

Wisdom Publications is the leading publisher of classic and contemporary Buddhist books and practical works on mindfulness. To learn more about us or to explore our other books, please visit our website at wisdomexperience.org or contact us at the address below.

Wisdom Publications
132 Perry Street
New York, NY 10014 USA

We are a 501(c)(3) organization, and donations in support of our mission are tax deductible.

Wisdom Publications is affiliated with the Foundation for the Preservation of the Mahayana Tradition (FPMT).